SEEING THE FAITHFULNESS OF GOD THROUGH
A HEARTBREAKING ADOPTION JOURNEY

Broken Dreams in Wounded Hands

JENNI
de VRIES

Ark House Press
arkhousepress.com

© 2023 JENNI DE VRIES

All rights reserved. Apart from any fair dealing for the purpose of study, research, criticism, or review, as permitted under the Copyright Act, no part may be reproduced by any process without written permission.

Scripture quotations marked (NIV) are taken from the Holy Bible, New International Version®, NIV®. Copyright © 1973, 1978, 1984, 2011 by Biblica, Inc.™ Used by permission of Zondervan. All rights reserved worldwide. www.zondervan.com The "NIV" and "New International Version" are trademarks registered in the United States Patent and Trademark Office by Biblica, Inc.™

Some names and identifying details have been changed to protect the privacy of individuals.

Cataloguing in Publication Data:
Title: Broken Dreams in Wounded Hands
ISBN: 978-0-6459207-1-0 (pbk)
Subjects: FAM004000 [FAMILY & RELATIONSHIPS / Adoption & Fostering]; REL012030 [RELIGION / Christian Living / Family & Relationships]; REL012170 [RELIGION / Christian Living / Personal Memoirs];
Other Authors/Contributors: de Vries, Jenni;

Design by initiateagency.com

Contents

Acknowledgments vii

Introduction ix

Chapter 1: Who am I? 1

Chapter 2: Hard Life Lessons in the Teenage Years 7

Chapter 3: Future Direction 17

Chapter 4: A Year of Service 25

Chapter 5: Family Life 37

Chapter 6: To say 'I do' or not to say 'I do'! 47

Chapter 7: In The Family Way 55

Chapter 8: Am I on My Own? 75

Chapter 9: The Need, The Desire 85

Chapter 10: Getting Going in More Ways than One 91

Chapter 11: Seeking Approval 105

Chapter 12: Looking forward 117

Chapter 13: Doubt 125

Chapter 14: Abraham's Lesson 133

Chapter 15: South Africa - A New Direction; or is it? 139

Chapter 16: Life Doesn't Slow Down 145

Chapter 17: Simply Trusting 149

Chapter 18: Fostering 155

Chapter 19: Fostering Stories 159

Chapter 20: Broken Dreams in Wounded Hands 163

Chapter 21: Hope - In What? 167

Epilogue 171

To Samuel, Mitchell, Justin and Darcy. May you all be able to see Gods faithfulness through the trials that come your way.

Acknowledgments

There are so many people who I'd like to thank for their input into my life and/or the completion of this book, starting with my mum and dad. My heart is heavy that you are not here with me to celebrate the publication of my story, but if not for your consistent faith in God and love and support of me until God called you home, I would never have had the courage to even consider adoption in the first place, and there wouldn't have been a story to write.

My husband, Nic. We've been through a lot together, the highest highs and the lowest lows; but you've never given up on us. Thank you for walking the road of adoption with me and helping me not to sink into the depths when the way became a quagmire.

My adult sons, Samuel, Mitchell, Justin and Darcy. Thanks for putting up with the challenges which adoption brought to our family. Being such amazing kids made the decision easy to want to have more. You may not remember, but your simple faith filled prayers for the adoption so often gave me the strength to keep going. I'm eternally grateful to the Lord for giving you to me for a while. You belong to him, yet he gave me the privilege of being your mum.

My sisters, Sally Westlake and Kathryn Birch. Thank you for being as excited about our adoption plans as we were. Your support and friendship have been and continue to be a great source of encouragement to me.

Sally, if you hadn't pushed me to publish, I don't think it would ever have happened. How blessed am I to have sisters who are the dearest of friends? From the bottom of my heart, thank you.

My niece, Pippa Dugmore. What a stunning piece of art you created for the book cover. Thank you so much for agreeing to come up with something. It's just perfect.

My daughter-in-law, brothers-in-law and all the Haeusler nieces and nephews, (take a deep breath!), Maygan, Geoff, Darren, Jerome, Josie, Trinity, Grace, Pippa, Cameron, Molly, Lara, Sophia, Laura and Ella. Thanks for your input (and fun banter) about what to use as my author name; Jennifer de Vries, Jenni de Vries, Jennifer M de Vries, Jenni M de Vries…. Who'd have thought it would be so hard!

My dear friend Wanda Cavanagh. You have been my confidante and faithful prayer partner for so many years. Thank you for your prayers, love, encouragement and friendship.

My editor and friend Bec Faricy. Who knew that only a year after moving to Kununurra I would have made a friend who would offer to edit my book? (Who knew I'd even be publishing a book!) Of course, God did, and I'm so grateful he brought us here and you across my path. What a tremendous gift you've given me. Thank you so much.

My co-publisher, Ark House. A heartfelt thanks to you all for working with such a rookie! From the get-go I was met with encouragement and enthusiasm about this project. John Philips, your initial emails gave me hope that my story might be worth publishing. James Newman, you made me feel welcome in the Ark House family; thanks for being so enthusiastic and easy to talk to. Nicole Danswan and all your team, all I can say is wow! The book looks beautiful.

Introduction

One mid-morning recently, my husband and I were chatting as we crossed paths in our bedroom when there was a loud "THUNK" sound from our window which made me jump. Oh no, a bird had flown into the glass! I rushed out to the verandah to see if the little fella had survived and saw a beautiful, bright blue, twitching little bird. It looked like it was gasping for breath and I thought for sure it must be going to die. Sam, our eldest son, was visiting and as an animal lover he picked up the little bird, which was actually a gorgeous, delicate Azure Kingfisher, and carried it inside. Well, the little tyke kept on breathing, and though it was very dazed, its eyes were still bright. Sam kept it warm in his hands and as it got stronger he took it outside and soon enough was able to release it and it eventually flew away.

I tell you this story as it reminds me of our hopes and dreams. Sometimes they're bright and fly hopeful and free, but then they crash into something hard, come crashing down and lie gasping for breath on the ground. But our God is a people-lover! He takes that little delicate twitching dream, and he warms it in his scarred hands, hands that know suffering and pain. Only he knows if it will die, or fly again, or if it will be the same or somehow changed. Either way, it is safe in his hands. I think Jesus' hands are the best place to put all our hopes and dreams, even all of ourselves, broken or otherwise. He knows what to do with them; he knows what to do with you.

Proverbs 19:21 (NIV)
"Many are the plans in a person's heart, but it is the Lord's purpose that prevails."

Chapter 1

Who Am I?

The time of year was just right. After my sister Sally was born in the height of summer (too hot!), then 19 months later Kathryn was born in August (too busy shearing!), I was born in April on Easter Saturday. Not too hot, not too cold, not too much busyness on the farm. Mum was hoping for me to wait until resurrection Sunday, but apparently I had other plans! I was to be the last of three girls. To this day I am grateful for my wonderful childhood. My dad was a farmer, and although by today's standards our farm was not big, it was more than enough to provide for our family. I loved living on the land. It was a quiet, turmoil-free life in the peace and calm of Wanneranooka Farm. Well, that's the perspective of a child. I'm sure the drought of the seventies and the ups and downs of farming life were not quite so tranquil for my Mum and Dad, but those things left me unaffected year after year.

Although I was not close to my sisters as a young child, we generally got on fairly well. Sally and I would come to loggerheads now and then, with one occasion in particular sticking in my memory. The whole family were in the car driving the 10km home from town, and Sally and I were bickering most of the way in the back. Dad got so sick of it that he kicked all three of us out when we were still about a kilometre from home. We were already on our driveway so it was a quiet walk. We quit bickering, but I don't think Kathryn was too impressed since she was just an innocent bystander! Sorry Kathryn! Isn't it funny the things which remain in our memory from our childhood?

There are many memories I hold dear, of things which defined who we were as a family, but nothing so much as the faith of my parents. My Dad had been raised in a Christian family with his father being very involved in the Uniting Church and his mother being the organist/pianist. My Mum became a Christian at the age of 19 after attending a tent mission in Bunbury, Western Australia. Her conversion was sure and certain, and she never looked back. They met and married at the age of 30 and about two years later Sally was born. The faith of my parents was not a Sunday church attendance thing. Sure, we went to church each Sunday, but it was a lot more than that. Their belief in and personal knowledge of the person of Jesus Christ led them to live a life of service. Dad was always very generous in his financial support of various Christian ministries and served as an elder in the Uniting Church of Three Springs, our hometown in Western Australia. Mum served the Lord in so many ways not the least of which was running the local Sunday School, the 'Jesus Team', and hosting many travelling Christian groups and others who needed a place to stay for as long as they were in town. Almost every evening after dinner we would read from the Bible as a family and pray together. My parents' faith was not theoretical; it had feet, legs and arms which carried my sisters and I until we could stand on our own.

That day came for me when I was 9 years old. We were down in Perth, for what, I can't remember, and we attended a church on Sunday as was our custom. Well, my life would never be the same again. I don't remember

WHO AM I?

a word that was preached in the service but what I do remember is that I didn't go out to the children's ministry, instead I stayed in the service with Dad and Mum, a divine direction I believe. When the minister had finished speaking, he asked if anyone would like to give their life over to Jesus, to trust in Him and to follow his example in life. I knew that God was asking me that same question and I felt compelled to respond. I put my hand up and went to the front with everyone else who responded that day. I don't recall any emotion, though I'm sure I felt emotional; I don't remember the prayers prayed for me, although I'm sure they were just what I needed; I can't recall what was spoken to me, although people did speak with me. What I do remember, as though it was yesterday, was that I knew I was a sinner, I knew Jesus was a real man who lived a real life and died a real death to rise to a real life so my sin could be washed away and I could be friends with God. I wanted nothing more but to serve Him for the rest of my life. I know it seems crazy for a 9-year-old to make such a firm decision, but I did; and although I've not always lived up to my desire to serve the Lord, I've never doubted him, even when things were hard.

Throughout those idyllic childhood years there were many times when my tender heart struggled with the reality of life. On the outside I was a happy-go-lucky little blond headed girl. I loved being with my family and spending time with my friends. I loved music and drama and I loved to watch TV! But on the inside I was often fearful. I would see a report of a war being fought in Iraq, and I would be afraid that somehow a plane would fly over and we would be bombed! It seems so ridiculous, but to me it was so real. I used to dream often, sometimes wonderful dreams, but it was the few recurring nightmares which I can still recall today. They would always leave me feeling a dread deep down inside. Then there was the time I saw footage of the famine which devastated Ethiopia. As a tender 8-year-old I was so terribly upset to see the bloated bellies of the children and the desperate pleas of their families, and wanted to do something. But what could I do? So, I said nothing and did nothing while my heart broke for my suffering brothers and sisters in that far away land. I didn't see skin colour, I didn't see race, I didn't see strange people; I just saw people who were like me who were suffering in such extreme circumstances. I thought that if I was born there that would have been the reality of life for me.

Yet the reality of my life was so very different. I was a good student at school and enjoyed learning new things, especially the piano and later the guitar. I'm sure I could have done better if I had done exactly what my piano teacher set for me to do, but I found the music lessons a bit dry. Not my teacher's fault, but I wanted something different. So, with the slowly growing skills I possessed on piano, I taught myself to play the pieces which I wanted to play. I would do a cursory practise of the set lessons, then dedicate my time to the ones I really wanted to play! I think it was just as well actually, as at the age of 12, with the encouragement of my parents, I applied for a music scholarship to one of the public music specialist high schools in Perth. Mum drove me two hours to the regional centre of Geraldton for two days of testing, both academic and musical. One of the tests was actually an audition, but somehow we were unprepared. I didn't have any music! How could this happen? I put it down to the ignorance of a 'country bumpkin'! The reality of my situation was kind of awkward.

Well, we didn't panic. That wasn't going to help. Maybe I could just play one of those favourite pieces which I'd taught myself. I knew it off by heart anyway! So, I played the first few pages of Fur Elise which I'd taught myself and adapted slightly so it was easier for me to play. Well, I think maybe that was the clincher for the assessor. A few weeks later we were informed that I had been successful and that if I chose to accept the scholarship I should come to Perth and visit the two schools which offered it, to choose which one I would attend. Never mind that Perth was 330 kilometres away. This

WHO AM I?

was the chance of a lifetime. To top it all off I had been a lover of orchestral music since as early as I could remember, especially the violin. Which instrument do you think I won the scholarship to learn? Of course, it was the violin! I think the Lord was doing something. Was it about the music though? Maybe, but as I see it from this side of the experience, I believe it was about a whole lot more. Learning to trust the Lord, holding on to Him when there was no one and nothing else to hold onto, truly giving my life over to Him. That's more what it was about.

Chapter 2

Hard Life Lessons in the Teenage Years

Talk about hard times though. I had no idea what was about to hit me! At 12 years of age, I was leaving home to board with a family I had only met once before. I was coming from a farm where I had lived my whole life with my 2 older sisters and a primary school of 120 students, to living in a city suburb with a family who had 3 boys, my age and younger, and going to a high school with 120 students in my year group alone! I had to navigate through city living, curious boys, intellectual house parents and a nominally Christian home. "God help me!" And so he did. Through prayer, reading the Bible, finding Christian friends and the music of Keith Green and others, I hung on to my saviour. One particular song became a staple when things were hard. It was called "He'll take care of the rest". The song spoke of Noah and Moses and others who were faced with trials which they didn't understand, yet they trusted in God who was always leading and guiding them. That was what I was challenged to do too; that was what I was determined to do.

BROKEN DREAMS IN WOUNDED HANDS

Yes, everyday life was not easy, but I was not alone. Jesus was the one constant who walked with me all the way. He was the only one who came with me from Three Springs when I moved to Perth. He was the only one who saw all my trouble. He was the only one who really knew what was going on in my life and in my heart. He was the only one who was always there. He brought good Christian friends into my life. He led me to a church and youth group where I was fed, challenged and nourished in my faith. Through all the ups and downs, he blessed me with the ability to express myself through song and when I was thirteen I penned the lyrics and tune to my first.

> *It was a dark and gloomy morning*
> *That the stranger came to town*
> *He was riding on a stallion big and strong*
> *And all the sky was dark*
> *Not a sound from near or far*
> *Just the gallant horseman's voice humming a song*
>
> *Then something lurched inside me*
> *As the stranger stopped outside*
> *And dismounted his well groomed thorough-bred*
> *But all my fear just melted*
> *Into a restful peace*
> *As the stranger tilted up his radiant head*
>
> *Then I heard him knock upon the door*
> *But I didn't move one step*
> *Afraid to let him in or shut him out*
> *But his knocking was consistent*

HARD LIFE LESSONS IN THE TEENAGE YEARS

Though I ignored his plea
And he didn't speak, didn't raise a shout

Finally I weakened
And when I let him in
I found out why he never went away
For he's the mighty prince of peace
The gallant son of God
The most high Jesus Christ to this day

And now I look back on those days
I left Him standing there
Out in the cold, knocking to come in
I pray one day your door will open
Cos' he's still knocking now
And with his great love you're always bound to win

Yes I pray one day your door will open
Cos' he's still knocking now
And with his great love you're always bound to win

Although I felt trapped in many ways, being so far from home and family, I was always free when I was singing to my Lord. Oh, how I was so grateful for his presence with me.

He'd also given me amazing parents who prayed for me every day. Parents who had the means and occasion to purchase a unit not far from my school so at age 14 and 8 months I could move in with my sisters. By his loving guidance I was able to serve Him through the church and youth group I attended. And he'd blessed me with sisters who became friends as we lived together. Living with family again was amazing. God surely was good to me. He never left me. He sustained me all the way, day by day.

Jesus was closer than a brother to me. I wanted others to know the incredible joy and peace which comes through placing your faith in Him, regardless of your outward circumstances. But I wasn't very good at sharing it. On the one hand I didn't care what people thought of me, but on the other hand, I had a terrible fear of being rejected. Oh, such a deep fear. As a result, I rarely shared the gospel with my non-Christian friends. To my shame I remained silent too often. May the Lord forgive my omission. I found it easier sharing the gospel with complete strangers when our youth group joined YWAM on short outreaches than I did with my friends. But God is so gracious and he kept the fire in me alight. He even inspired another song.

> *Some people throw away*
> *All their loves from childhood days*
> *But here's one love that will last forever*
> *The Lord Jesus and me together*
>
> *He helped me through both thick and thin*
> *When he died on the cross to save my sin*
> *And now I feel it's my turn Lord*
> *To pay you back for the weight you bore*
> *When carrying the worlds sins on your back*
> *In the form of a cross*
> *Up the beaten track*
>
> *Lord please warm my stone cold heart*
> *With your pure love that will never depart*

HARD LIFE LESSONS IN THE TEENAGE YEARS

Help me to be more like You
In everything I say and do
You helped me through........

Lord help me remember You're with me today
And that You will guide me wherever I stray
Help me not to look down when I'm sad
But to look to You instead, and be glad

That You helped me through.......

All I wanted to do was to serve Him. Although I had a funny idea of how he was going to use me! I had grown a passion not only for music and singing, but also for drama. What could I do with those talents to the glory of God? Of course, I'll study musical theatre at the academy of performing arts and focus on a career there. I could share the gospel with so many artists who needed a saviour as much as anyone! Well, what else would God have in mind? Just in case, I thought I'd better study hard enough to get a score on my final exams which would be good enough to get me into nursing in case the Lord wanted me to take that path. But I was pretty certain he didn't! No, musical theatre was the path for me. What? It was a great idea!

So, this is how it was. My heart was set in two directions, though I didn't know it at the time. One direction was to do my own thing, and the other was to do what God wanted me to do. Oh, I added God to my own thing, I was going to serve Him while fulfilling my desire for a career in musical theatre. But what did he really want me to do? Well, the answer started to come in a cryptic way when I was 15 years old. It was the summer holidays and some of the youth from our church had organised a bus to take whoever wanted to come from the youth group to a Christian conference in Adelaide. There were a couple of well-known speakers and it sounded like it would be an awesome event with thousands of people attending from all over Australia. My sisters and I, along with 18 or so others, crammed ourselves and our stuff into a coaster bus and bounced our way over 1500 km to cross the Nullarbor Plain to Adelaide, the capital of the state of South Australia. Well, the conference met all my expectations. It was amazing! But one experience I had there was more amazing still.

It happened that at the end of a meeting one evening I had gone forward for prayer. I was serious about my faith. I wanted my life to make a difference for the Lord. In that moment I was totally surrendered to the Lord. At some point while I was standing there, I felt the Lord speak to my heart. Although I heard no audible voice, it was as clear as the chiming of a bell on a still morning. "To serve me you will have to leave your family and friends." What? I began to cry. I'm 15! I can't leave my family and friends. How am I supposed to do that? But there you have it. I couldn't mistake it. It was so clear and it stayed with me for days, even weeks after. While I don't remember sharing it with anyone at the time, I did think about it in my heart often. A couple of months later, though not denying the message from the Lord, I had justified in my mind that the message was for some time in the distant future, after I'd finished my study and really had something to offer the Lord in service to Him. All I can say in hindsight is that God's ways are truly higher than our ways and his thoughts than our thoughts. This was made clear to me through a series of meetings at our church only 18 months later.

There was a song which was sung often at the time. It reflected words from Psalm 2:8 and Isaiah 6:8 which read – 'Ask of me, and I will make the nations your heritage, and the ends of the earth your possession.' and,

HARD LIFE LESSONS IN THE TEENAGE YEARS

'Then I heard the voice of the Lord saying, "Whom shall I send? And who will go for us?" And I said, "Here am I. Send me!"'.

I would stand with my eyes closed and my hands raised, singing with all my heart to the Lord. I was ready to hear his voice again. Maybe for this reason, when the call came at the conclusion of the service for people to come forward who wanted prayer, I felt compelled to go. I knew God wanted me to go forward as I would get butterflies in my stomach which wouldn't go away until I did! But I didn't know exactly what to ask for prayer for! So, for about 3 or 4 weeks I went forward for prayer. Various people I knew but whom I wasn't close to, prayed for me. Nothing spectacular happened. What was it all about? Obedience maybe? Would I be willing to follow the Lord's leading even if I didn't understand? I don't know, but I kept going forward.

Then one evening that still small voice spoke to me again. It had been 18 months since the last encounter, and now here it was once more. "I want you to go and it's going to be soon." The message hit me like a road train and again I began to cry. In my mind, since the last time the Lord spoke was only 18 months ago, 'soon' meant within 18 months! I sent up an arrow prayer for confirmation, "Lord if this really is You speaking to me, please send someone to pray for me who I know really well." I soon felt a hand on my shoulder. As I turned to see who had come to pray for me, I saw it was my sister, Sally! "Oh Sally", I cried, "The Lord wants me to go and it's going to be soon". I was looking for some gentle response to calm my unsettled heart. But God had sent Sally! "If he's told you to go, then you have to go!" Praise the Lord. He'd answered my prayer! Someone who I knew really well had come to pray for me, and she had confirmed that still small voice. But where to from here?

Well, the Lord was certainly calling the shots, so all I could do was to keep doing what I was doing, all the while listening in for the next direction from that still small voice. Actually, that's not quite as simple as it sounds. By this time I was coming near the end of my final year of high school and I had mock exams, then genuine exams to face. I half-heartedly worked at completing my school education. It was hard to focus. I didn't really know exactly what I was going to do after. Music and drama were still my main focus, so when my exams were over, Mum organised for an audition for me to the Western Australian Academy of Performing Arts to study musical theatre. It seemed to fit with my gifts and my desires for the future, but God had other plans which were to unfold quickly and decisively.

Well, the long-awaited day of my final year 12 exams rolled around. Phew! It was finally all over. Mum was down in Perth to support me through the exam period and she had a special treat in store for me that day. She picked me up from the school and said she was taking me somewhere special. Where on earth could that be though? I was not a lover of Perth, although for a city it's not too bad. But I'd just finished my exams. Where could I go to celebrate that? I just didn't know. To my utter surprise, I found myself walking up the gangway of a ship in port in Fremantle, about half an hour from where I was living. Wow, what is this place? My mind was spinning. The butterflies returned! God's cryptic directions were starting to become clear. Not totally in focus, but certainly less and less vague. God's words which I had pondered so often in the last couple of years were finally coming around to their conclusion.

So, I guess you'd like to know what was so special about the ship I was nervously walking the gangway to experience? It was called the MV Doulos and was operated by an interdenominational Christian organisation called Operation Mobilization. The word 'Doulos' is from the Greek and means 'servant'. It aptly described the 250 strong crew members who lived and worked onboard. They considered themselves servants of the Lord, called to serve Him by serving the nations of the world. The main area of minis-

HARD LIFE LESSONS IN THE TEENAGE YEARS

try was the selling and distribution of books from the extensive book shop onboard. One fifth of all the books in the shop were Christian books and the others covered many and varied subjects for children through to students, parents, teachers and even libraries. So why would I get so excited about books, and what was so special that my spine tingled?

Obviously selling books wasn't the only thing they did onboard the MV Doulos. Their chief goal was to bring life, help and hope to hurting, impoverished, soul weary people of the world. Books were one medium to achieve this, but there was so much more. They ran open air meetings and meetings onboard to present the good news of Jesus Christ through songs, stories, dramas, dances rope tricks and talks. Ship tours were conducted to introduce people to the lives and work of those onboard and to speak words of hope and encouragement. Teams were sent out at every port which was visited to do many and varied things such as visiting people in hospitals, schools, prisons and churches, volunteering with aid projects, encouraging local Christians in their faith and activities, distributing books and Christian literature to many who would not ever have access to such things otherwise, and on and on.

I don't know which of the above activities stirred my heart the most, but I knew this was the place for me! I convinced my Mum to take me to visit a second time. We toured the ship and found out a lot more about its ministry. We met some wonderful people and left with some brochures about the ship and how to join. I was sure that this was what the Lord had been leading me toward for the last 18 months, but really, what would I know about hearing from and following the Lord? Not much! But I knew from my Bible reading about Gideon. When he was given directions from the Lord, he sought confirmation. That's what I determined to do. I would do a Gideon and put out my proverbial 'fleece' to see how God would answer.

All I can say at this point is that God is so faithful. I didn't exactly know how God would respond to my requests, but I was excited to find out.

Actually, I had three 'fleeces' to put out. I determined that if even one of them were not answered, I would take it that God did not want me to go at this time. Well, the first two were answered within a week or two, but the third, nothing. In fact, the third request was really the clincher anyway. I had asked the Lord for not only the approval, but also the support of my parents. I wanted to honour them, so if they didn't think I should go, then I wouldn't go. At the same time I wasn't going to nag them for an answer. When I mentioned that I felt the Lord wanted me to join the Doulos my Mum had responded, "I can see you joining in a year or two, but I think it would be a good idea to get your study out of the way first, and then think about joining." Hmmm, but I was so sure this was the Lord's timing. I didn't say anymore, but I just waited.

I waited and I waited and I waited. Mum had gone back to Three Springs and I still hadn't an answer from them. I shared with Sally about my predicament. If I was going to join the Doulos, I had to be in Darwin, Australia, in just a few weeks, yet I still didn't have the approval of my parents. Sally suggested we pray together and I can picture it even now as I write. We went outside of our little unit and sat on the lawn in the shade to pray. As we finished the telephone rang. It was Mum! She wanted to speak to me. "Everywhere I turn I keep seeing the brochure about the Doulos. I can't get away from it. I think the Lord wants you to go!" Oh my gosh! Talk about an answer to prayer. I know the Lord always answers our prayers when we pray according to his will, but it's not always so quick! Doulos, here I come.

Chapter 3

Future Direction

Three weeks is about all the time I had to get myself organised for a three-month stint of service on the MV Doulos. It was all a bit crazy. At the very least plane tickets and packing had to be sorted. Thankfully I had a current passport as I had gone on a music tour with the school choir to England and Wales just a couple of years before. As I was joining in Darwin, Australia, I didn't need to worry about visas. At this point I was so grateful for my parents' support. This was not a free venture in the least. My parents were always wise with their finances and had put money aside to help in the purchase of my first car. I asked if I might be able to use that money to fund this mission trip and they both agreed. Although I can't remember the details of how it all came together, I'm pretty sure my parents would have arranged it. From applying to join the crew, to buying the tickets, to transport to the airport, to arranging the money, they sorted it all. Without their involvement, it never would have happened. They were serving on the mission field through me, there's no doubt about that. I'm pretty sure that they saw things which I didn't at the time. This was a pivotal moment in the future of my life, yet I didn't see it until much later.

Remember that I was intent on studying musical theatre and using that as a springboard to serve the Lord? Well, my Mum had previously organised an audition for me at the Academy of Performing Arts. The twist was that the day I had to be onboard the Doulos was the same day as the audition. The crossroad was before me. I was excited to go on the Doulos and serve the Lord there, but I thought at the time that in doing so I was giving up my deep desire to be a musician and performer on stage. That was okay with me. God had been working on my heart about dying to my own desires and living for Him for many years. I saw this as a very practical outworking of that call. I would leave my desire to perform at the foot of the cross of Christ. I didn't know how he wanted me to serve Him except at this point to join the Doulos, but I knew that he was leading me; all I could do was trust Him for the rest.

There was certainly a lump in my throat and butterflies in my stomach as I waved goodbye to my parents and friends at the airport in Perth. God was leading an unadventurous country girl of 17 to a place I had never been, to live with people I had never met, to do what I didn't know! Yet somehow, through the tears and the nervousness, there was an excitement and a deep peace. I was heeding the call. I was leaving my family and friends to serve Him. That's just what he'd said he wanted me to do. Yet I had not sought it, or tried to figure out how to do it. He'd done it all. I guess that's often how he works with the young in their faith. I felt like I was in the boat, but God was manning the oars. I was happy to be carried along to wherever he wanted me to go. In a very practical sense I was going to Darwin and then sailing on to the Solomon Islands and Papua New Guinea, but in a spiritual sense, I was dying to myself to have my life given back to me. And that he did. Our God is so gracious and compassionate

FUTURE DIRECTION

and kind. I made new friends from many nations of the world, I was able to use my musical and drama abilities in direct service of Him and he was showing me a pattern by which I could live my life on into the future.

Finally I had found my place in the world. Three months was just not enough. Before I left I was encouraged to think about committing for a year or two. For me it was a no-brainer. Of course I wanted to come back. After aeroplane trouble in Papua New Guinea I had to fly the long way home, again organised by my Mum and Dad. I flew from Lae to Goroka to Port Moresby to Cairns to Brisbane to Sydney to Melbourne to Perth and finally was driven home to Three Springs. It was all quite surreal, but I knew where I was headed. I talked it over with Dad and Mum and they agreed to let me work on the farm in the family business while I sorted things out to go back on the Doulos. The world was waiting and I had to prepare for it.

For most of 1992 that's exactly what I did. I helped on the farm and in the homestead and saved every penny I earned to pay for my return. It wouldn't be enough though. This being the case I also sought sponsors who would be willing to support me financially while I was away. Isn't it funny how things work out? I had been involved in the ministry of a large church in Perth for five years, yet when I approached them, they declined to support my mission venture. Yet several people from the small country Christian fellowship which I was a part of back home in Three Springs whole-heartedly got behind me. It was humbling to think that these people who really only knew me through my parents were so willing to help me out. I guess they could see that in supporting me, they were actually helping to fulfil the Lord's great commission to "go into all the world and preach the gospel". Along with my Mum and Dad, they were joining me on the mission field without having to leave home. As God was calling me to go, he was also calling them to support me, and that's exactly what they did.

As a requirement of Operation Mobilisation, the ministry of which the Doulos was a part, I had to complete some particular training. In my case, I travelled to Taiwan to attend a two-week course on missions and evangelism and two weeks service on the field. This was quite a testing time for me. The course was fabulous, held in a very picturesque mountainous region of Taiwan. But the weeks of service stretched me considerably. I was placed in a team in which I was the only English speaker, and being the typical Aussie that I am, English was the only language I could speak! There was a lady and a man from Hong Kong, a lady from Taiwan and two men from South Korea. The team leader was the man from Hong Kong. He spoke a spattering of English. The young lady from Hong Kong spoke English quite well, but she was very shy and didn't engage in conversation at all. Not to mention the locals in the village we stayed in. It was quite remote and only Taiwanese and dialects were spoken. It was a very quiet outreach from my end! It was at this time that I composed another song:

> When time is going slow
> And sometimes I feel so alone
> I remember all those times when
> You promised me You'd be with me
> You said, "Now don't you worry girl
> Daddy's always here
> I'm watching you in all you do
> There's no need for you to fear
>
> But still I have those times when
> I don't know what to do
> I try to pray and seek God's face
> But somehow I just can't break through

FUTURE DIRECTION

And so I just breakdown and cry
I don't know what to do
Or who to turn to
Who can I turn to
Who can I turn to

Then I hear this still small voice
It whispers my name
"I've been here all along", he says
I can feel your pain

And he says
"Don't you worry girl
Daddy's always here
I'm watching you in all you do
There's no need for you to fear
Don't you fear"

    I have often sang this song over the years and still today it rings true for me in so many ways. It has always been a challenge to keep my eyes on Jesus and not on the difficulties around me. I can relate to Peter walking towards Jesus on the water, then suddenly noticing the storm and starting to sink. Oh, I am so much like Him. Praise the Lord that he is willing and able to pull us up out of the overwhelming waters. At times the required training was just that: overwhelming.

    But my heart and mind was set on the goal of serving onboard the Doulos again, so I weathered the training and went back home to work and wait for the right time to leave again. By this time I was 18, and though still not an adventurer at heart, I had a passion inside which was burning intensely. By January 1993 I was ready to go. Again, I waved goodbye to my family and friends at Perth airport. This time the lump in my throat felt like a grapefruit! I was leaving for a whole year. So much could happen in that time. People change and move on, advance in different directions, even forget you. It was all in the Lord's hands. He's strengthened me to this point, I was sure he would not leave me in the cold now. And I was right! An encounter on an aeroplane and in an airport on the way made that very clear. I don't know if it was an angel in the form of a man, or just a man placed there by God to help me. But I know God was clearly working through him.

Do you want to know what happened? It occurred something like this. During the flight, I had a wonderful conversation with the man sitting next to me. He was a businessman from South Africa and seemed quite fascinated with my impending service trip on the Doulos. We talked about that and many other things. Our flight terminated in Kuala Lumpa Malaysia, where I had to stop overnight in transit before catching my next flight which would take me to Sri Lanka where the Doulos was in port. To help me out, a contact in Operation Mobilisation had given me the name and phone number of someone in K.L. who they believed would be willing to put me up for the night. When I'd disembarked from the plane and collected my luggage, I made a beeline for a public phone (no mobiles in those days!). The person who answered the phone said they were sorry but they couldn't help out. I hung up the phone with a trembling hand and a sinking feeling inside. What was I going to do? I had nowhere to stay and no money to make any international calls to Australia to seek advice. I was faced with sleeping in the terminal. Not a very exciting prospect to say the least! What happened next, however, I believe could only have been orchestrated by God.

FUTURE DIRECTION

I turned from the phone feeling like I was going to cry when who do you think should walk by? It was the man I had sat next to on the plane. I had told him during the course of our conversation that I had a contact who would look after me for the night in K.L., so when we'd disembarked, we'd said our goodbyes and gone our separate ways. Now, just by chance, in a crowded airport with thousands of people wandering here and there, he came walking by me. Divine appointment? I think so! He stopped when he saw me and asked how I went with the contact I'd been given. I explained that it didn't work out and that I wasn't sure what I was going to do. He immediately took me onboard. He knew K.L. well as he'd travelled there some considerable number of times. My situation had taken a turn for the better, it was all going to work out.

The wonderful man, a stranger really, hailed me a taxi. But he didn't just give me directions and leave me to it. He got in with me, directed the driver to a back-packers lodging, paid the driver and gave me cash to cover a night's stay there. Then he gave me clear directions regarding when and where to catch a taxi to get back to the airport for my connecting flight in the morning. Then he was off. I stood watching him go in another taxi thinking that maybe, just maybe, I had encountered an angel. At no time did I feel unsafe with this man. He was easy to talk to, he immediately jumped in to help when I desperately needed it, and I never saw him again. If he wasn't an angel but just a stranger, I wonder if he knew that he was a tremendous instrument of God to me that day. I guess I'll never know.

So you see, God was still with me, helping me, leading me, guiding me in so many practical ways. How could I not trust Him more and more? I'm fickle, that's why! Only a day later when I was waiting for another contact that wasn't where they were supposed to be in the airport in Sri Lanka, I got that sinking feeling again! Had I learnt nothing? I guess I'm just a bit slow to learn in the trusting area. Sure enough I found the people I was supposed to meet, some whom I had met in Taiwan five months earlier, and they took me to the Doulos. Yes, I had finally made it. Only for one night mind you. There was more training, pre-ship training, I had to complete onshore in a place called Kandy in Sri Lanka! I was driven there by a crew member along with another new recruit who was joining from the Philippines. Her name was Maria Cecilia Ibanios Verana. We were chalk and cheese, but were to become life-long friends. My year of foreign mission service had finally begun. Praise the Lord!

Chapter 4

A Year of Service

How can I aptly detail this life-changing year in just one chapter? Key moments should do it. So, I completed the pre-ship training and was soon sailing to my first port as a crew member from Colombo, Sri Lanka, to the Seychelles, an archipelago of 115 islands in the Indian Ocean, off East Africa. Oh, I can hear your thoughts, "Mission service my foot! Tropical paradise retreat more like it!" Well, this couldn't be further from the truth. I had been allocated a job in the Book Exhibition. Our tasks were varied. We could be asked to greet people as they came up the gangway to visit, or man the tills, or work in the little souvenir shop, or collect books from the holds in the bowels of the ship to replace books which had been sold, or take stock of/restock books on shelves. In the Seychelles this is what kept us working till the wee hours of the morning. Who would have thought that the local schools and libraries would want to be stocking their shelves while emptying ours?

It turned out that books were hard to come by in the Seychelles so our shelves were emptied out by every evening. That meant that we had to make sure the shelves were fully restocked by opening time the next morning. Down to the hold we went to bring out box after box of books. Then all the books had to be sorted and stacked on the shelves. By about one o'clock in the morning we would finally finish and drag our tired feet down to our cabins to bed. Unfortunately for us, there were two shifts in the book exhibition. One was the morning/evening shift, the other was the afternoon shift. I was working the morning/evening so after going to bed around 1:30 am I had to be showered, dressed, breakfasted and back on deck at 8:45 the next morning. All in all, it was a tough start to my year on the Doulos.

Although the first week was so challenging, it was also exhilarating! I had already made some good friends, and living and working with Christian young people who were of the same mind and heart as me was all I had hoped it would be. The best, however, was yet to come. I was just about to find out where the ship would be spending most of her time while I was a crew member. After serving onboard for three months or so, previously I had gleaned that the Doulos spent most of her time sailing the oceans around Asia. This certainly was the case. But not for the 12 months I was to be onboard. Remember that little girl, watching the famine unfolding in Ethiopia? Well, she was about to be reminded how much she had longed to go to Africa.

We left the Seychelles very tired but with a nine-day voyage ahead to recuperate. Actually, Book Exhibition staff were reallocated jobs during voyages as obviously there were no visitors to tend to. But the hours were predictable and the pace a lot slower. My heart didn't beat slower however. I had found out that the ship would be sailing for Kenya, Africa! Each day at sea brought me a day closer to the continent that had been deep in my heart for ten years. Not only were we stopping in Kenya, but for eleven of the twelve months I was to be onboard, we would be in Africa. From Kenya we were to sail to South Africa, then Mozambique, then Tanzania. I couldn't believe it. Africa! It was the place of my dreams. I was apprehensive about finally getting there. What if it was terrible? Or not what I expected. Well, God knew. I believe he'd burdened my heart at a tender age for such a time as I was about to enter. He'd been preparing me for this journey which would heal and refine a new heart in me.

There was no need for me to be concerned about how I would feel. The moment I stepped foot on African soil in Mombasa, Kenya I knew this was what I had been longing for all along. I got to know a local lady whose name was Olive. She was volunteering on the Doulos while it was in port. She was so lovely. On my day off she took me to the local zoo and showed me around her city. My eyes, ears and nostrils were filled with the sights, sounds and smells of Kenya and I just soaked in every minute of it. I felt like I had come home!

While we were there, I had the opportunity to share of the love of Christ with a young lady who had turned her back on Islam and had embraced a relationship with Jesus Christ. Understandably she was afraid of the reaction of her uncle. She came onboard with her head covered and her eyes lowered. What could I say to help her out? I was just an 18-year-old Aussie girl who had no experience in witnessing to Muslims, let alone counselling a young lady who had just left Islam. To this day I don't remember what I said to this precious, new Christian lady. What I do remember is that just before the Doulos was to sail from Mombasa, this lady came onboard again and met up with me. Her demeanour was substantially changed. Previously her head had been covered, but now her scarf hung loose around her shoulders. Her eyes had been downcast on our first meeting but now they shone clear and bright. She had been set free from fear. It had been fear which had bound her and cast her down, but Christ had released her from those chains. The joy which flowed from her was palpable. What a great God we serve. He did it all. I did nothing but witness his work in this lady's life.

BROKEN DREAMS IN WOUNDED HANDS

All in all, we spent about three weeks in Kenya, but I knew that I would never forget my first African experience and the people who had impacted on me in that beautiful land. I lost contact with Olive and the young Christian lady. I hope to meet them again in heaven one day and hear the story of the rest of their lives. For now, we were off to our next port, East London, South Africa. This would be a totally different African experience. This country would become a place I would long to come back to, a place which would be as dear to me as Australia itself. All, I believe, for the purposes and glory of the Lord. My love for South Africa and her people has not diminished from that day to this. It certainly left an indelible mark on me for life.

The connection began even before I set foot on this vast and varied land. As we came near the coastline, I could see rows of eucalyptus trees swaying in the coastal breeze. It looked like home! We were welcomed warmly by the locals in every port we visited, but none more than in Cape Town, with good reason too. The Doulos was to stay in port for about five months! This was very unusual, as our longest stay in a port was usually only about three or four weeks. In Cape Town, the ship had to go into dry dock so some work could be done. Although it was not unusual for the Doulos to enter a dry dock each year for maintenance, on this occasion some major electrical work needed to be done. The whole ship needed to be gutted and the wiring updated to change it from direct current to alternating current and to bring it up to international standards. All the male crew members were allocated work detail onboard the ship while all the women were placed in teams and sent out to work with various churches all over South Africa.

During my time there, I was blessed to have been placed in a team with my dearest friend onboard, Cecilia. Together with our teams we participated in open air meetings, youth meetings, church services, evangelism training, door to door ministry, school visits and so much more. The tools of our ministry were dramas, songs, sketch-boards, mimes, rope tricks, clowning and talks, among other things. We were billeted in families who attended Dutch Reformed churches, coloured churches and university campus churches in the Cape along with Evangelical English churches, Pentecostal inner-city churches and Baptist Indian churches of Durban in Kwazulu Natal. We also volunteered as cooks and cleaners at a training and outreach conference called "Love Southern Africa" which sent teams out all over South Africa and other southern African countries. This was a time of much learning and growing in my personal faith. I had come to reach others with the good news of Jesus, but all along, the Lord was changing me into the woman he wanted me to become.

Two experiences stood out during my time in South Africa, helping me to see faith in a different light. The first was being billeted by a particular family with whom I am still in contact today, the du Plessis'. I know this is a very common Afrikaner name, but Elaine and Louise were not your stereotypical Afrikaners. They were a beautiful, gentle family living in the coastal area of Summerset West. They welcomed me into their family as one of their own. Watching on, I could see that they shared the love of Christ with whoever came their way. They treated the young lady who came to help around the home and the young man who came to tend their garden as no different from themselves, even though their lives as white and black South Africans were polar opposites. These people helped me to see that it wasn't the style of church you attended which had any significance at all, but how you lived out your faith.

Let me explain. My last few years of high school I was involved in a very charismatic church. The singing was vibrant with the entire congregation joining in and clapping or toe tapping along. There were also times of gentle, quiet singing with many people raising their hands in surrender to the Lord and singing their own quiet songs of praise to Him while the musicians played a few repeated chord progressions. It was a most beautiful time where I could forget about all that was going on in my life and totally surrender myself in praise of Jesus and all he had done for me. At the time I thought that there was no other way to really come close to God. I cringe even now as I write this, but I was certainly a one-eyed charismatic who felt like you couldn't really be that close to the Lord unless you had that kind of freedom in worship. How wrong I had been. I didn't really understand what true worship was at all. The du Plessis family were involved in a very traditional Dutch Reformed church, no hand clapping or hand raising there, just your traditional hymns. Yet they were doing their best to live a life which was pleasing to the Lord and were, all the while, seeking his kingdom and his righteousness. The love of God was so evident in their lives. They were worshipping God with their lives. I was starting to learn that just as you can't put God in a box, neither can you put his followers in a box.

My time serving in the du Plessis' church and many others showed me that it really wasn't at all about how you expressed your faith at church services, but what you did with it all the rest of the time. Some Christians were very traditional and formal in their church services, yet their eyes shone with the love and hope of Christ. Others from those same churches had dull and lifeless eyes and valued the things of this world more highly than the things of the Lord. By the same token, I served in some very Pentecostal churches, where people prayed loud and long, where many spoke in unknown tongues and the preaching would be fervent and frantic. In these churches I found exactly the same thing as in the traditional churches. Some people were alive with the gospel of Christ, yet others were just going through the motions, be it very loudly! What a humbling experience. I was challenged to look into my heart and examine what I found there; to look at my Christian brothers and sisters with different eyes and to see them as the Lord does, not through my 'one-eyed charismatic' glasses!

The second experience which has left a lasting impression on me occurred when I was serving on a team in Durban. It happened that I had come down very sick with a fever. Unfortunately, at this time we were not being billeted by a family, but were camping out on the grounds of the church we were serving in. With this in mind, the team leader didn't feel it would be a good idea to leave me alone in the building while they went off to an evening event, so I was bundled up in the back of the bus and off we went. We were soon parked on a hillside just outside Durban and had met with some of the local Zulus to show the Jesus film. Sadly, the team were having technical problems with the projector and the gear, so the film was delayed. In the meantime, quite a crowd had gathered. My fever seemed to be getting worse and worse as I lay shivering in the back of the bus. What happened next made me wonder if I had died and gone to heaven! No, I still felt sick so it couldn't have been that! As the crowd waited for the technical problems to be sorted out, they started to sing. Have you ever heard the Zulu people sing? I was transported to some other place. Instead of making a fuss, whinging, complaining or walking away in annoyance, the people had started to sing. They sang in Zulu, so I couldn't understand the words, but the Lord ministered to my sick body as they sang. I was reminded right then, that as Christians, our response to trials should be to lift our voices in song. To paraphrase scripture, the Lord offers us oil of joy for mourning and a garment of praise for the spirit of despair (Isaiah 61:3). Aching, shivering and feverish, bundled up in the back of a bus parked on a dark hillside I joined the crowd and lifted my heart in singing praise to God.

There is so much more I could tell of my time in South Africa; like the time I was partnered with an English girl to go door to door to share the gospel with whoever would give us time. At one house the lady didn't speak English and neither my partner nor I could speak Afrikaans, yet somehow my partner and the lady understood each other, and the gospel was communicated clearly. Miraculous! Then there was the time when my parents came over to visit and surprised me by bringing my sisters with them. I was flabbergasted and probably made a fool of myself constantly hugging them and muttering my unbelief that they were there! On another occasion I had to share my testimony and I felt like the Lord wanted me to share a very painful and personal experience I had as a young teenager. In tears and with trembling, I obeyed the Spirit's prompting. As it turned out, there was a young teenage girl in the meeting who had had a similar, although far worse, experience of her own. After hearing my testimony, she felt able to talk about it for the first time and to seek help to find healing. These are a drop in the ocean of experiences I had in South Africa, maybe I should write a book about that someday!

For now though, we will leave South Africa. After sailing from Cape Town we visited Port Elizabeth and things returned to normal regarding working and ministry onboard. That is, we worked for five days in our allocated job, had one day where we were sent out on a ministry team and had one day off. After Port Elizabeth, all the crew were showing their fatigue. It had been a fruitful time in South Africa, but very tiring. With that in mind, the leaders onboard Doulos organised what they called a Sabbath Week in Richards Bay. Only a skeleton crew worked on the essential tasks, rotating with others so everyone got a break. We had a guest speaker who came in from the UK for 5 days and we were able to spend time together singing, praying and being fed from God's word. It was a wonderfully unifying time of refreshment and encouragement. Too soon, it seemed, it was over, and we were sailing out of South Africa for good.

A YEAR OF SERVICE

We didn't travel far, however, just to Mozambique for some totally different ministry work. We were sent out into the countryside to work on an agricultural team as well as encourage the local church. It felt good to work physically hard in the field with some of the local women. People were hungry for the literature which we had brought along to distribute, and they crowded around to make sure they didn't miss out on getting some. The times of singing in the small church were amazing too. It all lasted for two weeks, and then we were on our way to our last port of call in Africa, Tanzania.

Tanzania was very hot and humid, but the enthusiasm of the locals didn't seem to be dampened by the weather. They came in droves to wander around the book exhibition and to tour the ship. I tried to make the most of every ministry opportunity, as this was the last ministry port I was to visit during my time on the Doulos. In my spare time I joined in some onboard meetings with my dear friend Cecilia, and we performed some evangelistic dramas and shared about the work of the Doulos. An opportunity came up to join with a team who were doing some basic health training related to HIV AIDS in one of the local community centres, so I jumped at the chance and joined them for a day. All too soon our time in Africa drew to a close.

The voyage from Tanzania to Sri Lanka was eleven days, about as long as they come. I grieved that I was leaving the continent of my dreams, but as we sailed away, I felt sure that someday I would come back. Maybe for ministry, maybe to live, maybe to visit; I didn't know. But God knew, and my life was in his hands. It was a blessing to be able to spend so much time on my final voyage with the friends I had made over the past twelve months. We sang together, prayed together, and talked about our lives and our hopes for the future. My closest friends were from several different countries, including the Philippines, the UK, the Netherlands, Germany and Papua New Guinea. I didn't know if I would ever see them again this side of heaven. I hoped with all my heart that I would, but I held onto the fact that we would all be together in heaven one day and we could rejoice with the angels never to be separated again. I'm still longing for that day. For now, however, I had to set my sights for home. God wasn't finished with me yet. There was much more to do. I was sad to leave my friends and the wonderful work of Operation Mobilisation, but I was excited to encourage my Christian friends back home and to seek God's direction for my future. There was just one more serious test of faith I had to face before getting home. It came at an airport in India. As is the case in most missionary ministries, flights would always have to be the cheapest they could come by. This meant that they were not usually the most direct route or the most reliable airlines! With this in mind, I had to fly from Sri Lanka to India before getting a connecting flight to Malaysia, then another one to Perth. Sounds straight forward, but getting home would not be quite as easy as that.

Firstly, I didn't know that at the airport in Sri Lanka I had to go out to the hanger to check that my luggage had been checked in to the right plane! Thankfully, another passenger asked if I'd double checked my luggage and explained what I had to do. I quickly found it and made sure it was in the right place. Then when we got on the plane, which was disconcertingly hot and sticky inside, there came onboard an official who said that there was someone onboard who shouldn't be. Oh no, that couldn't be me, could it? Thankfully not, but I was concerned just the same! Finally, the plane took off and soon landed safely in India. Now all I had to do was go through customs, pick up my luggage and wait in the transit lounge for my next flight in a few hours. I was emotionally drained and exhausted so a few hours to rest sounded wonderful. But it wasn't to be.

A YEAR OF SERVICE

When I arrived at customs, I was taken aback that they wouldn't let me through on account of the fact that I didn't have a visa. What?! I only needed to go through and get my luggage, I had no intention of leaving the airport, let alone the baggage collection area. I showed the customs officer the ticket for my connecting flight, but it made no difference. He asked to see my passport as well. I obliged but my heart sank when he took it and my ticket and walked away into the office with it. I waited for him to come back. Others were going through. I waited some more. There weren't many left now. I still waited. Now I was alone in the customs area. What should I do? I could only pray. I didn't know anyone in India, I didn't have any contact numbers, I didn't have any currency. I wasn't exaggerating when I say I could only pray.

The minutes seemed like hours until wondrously someone came out from the offices. It was not the man who had taken my passport, but this man indeed had my passport and my airline ticket. Kindly he approached me and introduced himself. He handed over my documents and took me by the arm. "Let's get your luggage, shall we?" his voice was warm and reassuring. He led me through the customs and helped me with my luggage. He collected if for me and checked it in. Then he showed me to the transit lounge where I could sit comfortably and wait for my connecting flight. He even asked if I was hungry and brought a meal in for me. Soon enough I found myself sitting on the plane headed for Malaysia. The rest of the journey was uneventful. As I reflect on this time, it's clear the Lord had started and finished my mission service by sending a stranger to help me. Trusting only in Him is what it is all about. I can do all sorts of great things in his service, but it all must begin with a resolute trust in Him. I'm still learning this lesson today, but one thing that I know for sure: I have a wonderful God, and had an amazing end to an incredible year.

Chapter 5

Family Life

What a strange experience it was to be home again. Where did the year go? I would go for walks down the track, through the bush and around the paddocks and everything looked exactly the same. Yet somehow, everything was so different. I didn't think I would be home very long. I had received an invitation to go back to a church in Durban, South Africa and work with the youth. I also had hopes of studying at an international Bible School in England. At this point in time though, I needed to work, renew friendships, encourage my supporters and pray and search the scriptures. Prayer had to be the key. If God wasn't leading me, I didn't want to go. But it wouldn't be like last time. Previously the call to go had been so clear. Now I felt the Lord gently leading me to study his Word and choose for myself what he would be pleased for me to do. Hmmm, this was new. My prior experience wasn't going to help me here!

As I was trying to do all these things, I resumed my work on the farm and enjoyed spending time with some old and new friends from the church in Three Springs and surrounding towns. I also kept in touch with my closest friends from the Doulos. I mostly wrote letters or recorded messages on cassette tapes, (I'm showing my age here!), but occasionally we would speak on the phone. I also had the opportunity to join a Youth With A Mission (YWAM) team as a representative of OM for a tour of central and south Western Australia. Our goal was to encourage the churches to see beyond their doors to the need in the world; the need for knowledge, help and hope; to show them through God's word his desire for their full surrender of their lives to Him. This tour lasted only a few weeks, yet one small, seemingly insignificant and actually quite inconvenient event in the middle of it would change the course of my life forever.

This is how it transpired. I had been asked by the Assemblies of God church in Geraldton to present a drama at one of their services. Well, I was happy to agree and set about writing a solo drama which could be performed there. It wasn't for some time and in the meantime I had the invite to join with YWAM. Now the tour took us 740km to the goldfields town of Leonora, then 235km to Kalgoorlie, 390km on to Esperance, 187km to Ravensthorpe and finally 293km to Albany on the south coast, including several country towns in between. The catch was that I had to be in Geraldton to perform the drama in the middle of the tour. We all agreed that, as this was a previous engagement, I would leave the team from Ravensthorpe and rejoin them in Albany. While this doesn't sound too interesting, it was quite a crazy week. I travelled on a bus for about 820km back to Three Springs, then was driven 200km to Geraldton the next day by my parents where the drama went off without a hitch. Afterwards we were enthusiastically invited by Nic, a young man with a strange eye, to join him and some others for a milkshake at a local cafe before heading the 200km back to Three Springs. We gratefully agreed but only stayed for a short while before heading off. The day after that I was back on a bus to Albany, travelling 710km, to rejoin the YWAM team! What was that really all about - almost 2000km for a 5-minute drama? Yet the chance encounter with the young man would lead to so much more!

I finished the tour and eventually arrived back home. Soon after, I received a letter from the young man who had asked my parents and I to join him and the others after church. We had had a cursory chat when we had met, but not much more. The truth of the matter was that I wasn't sure who this Nic was. "Nic, Nic, Nic. Which one was Nic? Oh, that's right. He was the one with the odd-looking eye!" So I'd figured out who he was, now for the letter. In it, he mentioned that he enjoyed the drama and that it was nice to have met me. He would like to catch up some time if I was in Geraldton again, but if not, he wished me well. As it happened, I was already planning on going to visit the AOG church in Geraldton the next Sunday anyway, so I thought I would thank him in person when I saw him at the service. What I didn't know, is that he was a shift worker and wasn't always able to attend church. No matter, I just asked Chris, one of the pastors who was a good friend, to thank Nic for the letter, if he happened to see him at all. Although I didn't notice at the time, I'm sure there was a sparkle in his eye as he eagerly agreed. There must have also been a cheeky little thought in the back of his mind which was about to become an action!

Much later I found out that Chris had not waited until he saw Nic next, but he'd enthusiastically called him that day and passed on my thanks for the letter in tones that suggested I was keen to meet him again! Apparently that was all Nic needed to pluck up the courage to call me on the phone himself. It so happened then, that a couple of days after I'd spoken to Chris, I had a phone call from Nic asking me if I'd like to go out to dinner with him! Of course he couldn't know that I lived about 200km from Geraldton on a farm, so after accepting his invitation I asked him where he would like to meet in Geraldton. He quickly replied that he was more than happy to come and pick me up. Umm, he really didn't get how far away I was.

When I explained, he was undeterred, he was adamant that he would like to come to Wanneranooka and pick me up. Well, knock me over with a feather! That's a significant investment in time and money to get to know someone he may not even like! I decided then and there that if he was willing to come and get me, he must be worth getting to know a bit better! I was determined however that I was not going to try and impress this man. When he arrived, he would find me dusty and in my work clothes helping out with draughting sheep. That might test his resolve. I could only wait and see how enthusiastic he was after seeing me like that.

Little did I know that Nic didn't hold delicate girls in high regard, but had a strong leaning towards girls who weren't afraid to get their hands dirty with some hard physical work! Hmm, box one was ticked for him, I think! As I'd organised to have half the day off, I finished my work not long after Nic arrived and got ready to head off. He had a special afternoon and evening planned. All the while I was observing what kind of man this Nic was. He played some of my favourite Keith Green music in his car on our way to Geraldton and whistled along to some of the songs. The thought crossed my mind, "He's whistling in tune. That's a bonus for a music lover like me!" Now he'd ticked one of my boxes! How many more ticks would we give each other before the end of the day? We were about to find out.

The first place Nic took me was to a place which has become my favourite spot in the mid-west, Ellendale Pool. It's a deep, permanent pool of water which is part of the Greenough River. It has a stunningly beautiful and rugged cliff on one side, and is flat on the other so you can drive up to the water's edge. At the time I didn't even know this place existed! I'm not sure how I could have lived in the mid-west most of my life and never come across it, but here it was. That was another box ticked for me. If Nic bought me to this place, then he must like the scrappy Aussie bush and its peaceful billabongs just as I do. We went swimming there before Nic took me back to his place where we were able to change and get ready for dinner. This was my first ever dinner date and Nic was pulling out all the stops. He took me to quite a fancy restaurant by the ocean front in the centre of Geraldton, a relaxing place to eat dinner and view the sun setting gracefully over the water.

It was dark when we had finished our meal and it was time to go home. Usually that would be the end of a date, but we still had a two-hour drive back to Wanneranooka! A lot of conversation and contemplation can occur on just such a drive, and a lot of both did! I don't remember exactly what time we arrived back to the farm, but it was quite late. My Mum and Dad were still up and given the late hour they asked Nic if he would like to spend the night rather than turn tail and head straight back to Geraldton. Since he'd already driven almost 400km for our date, he gratefully accepted the offer and was shown to the guest room. It had been an interesting day, from dusty sheep yards, to a cool water hole, to a sunset dinner on a 400km round trip! I was tired as my head hit the pillow. Although my eyelids were heavy for sleep, my heart had been stirred. Spending the last 10 hours or so with Nic had not put me off, but had left me wanting to know this man more. Over time, that's just what I would do.

As a matter of fact, Nic and I would get to know each other very well in a very short space of time. As he was a shift worker, he would come and visit for a few days at a time. I still had to work, but he was happy to tag along or just hang out at the farm. He seemed to enjoy helping out with some farm labour too. When you spend so much time with someone, you get to know them much more fully than you do if you only go out a couple of nights a week! One occasion though showed me a side of Nic which impressed me very deeply. He was staying at the farm on one of his rostered days off when I received a devastating phone call. A good friend of mine from the Doulos, Bombi, had just passed away. He had previously been diagnosed with kidney disease, but he was from the Philippines and treatment options were not great. his prospects had seemed hopeful with the right treatment, but it was not to be, and he died due to kidney failure. I was so upset. A young man in his early twenties shouldn't be dying. He was so full of life. Cheeky and lovable with a heart desiring to honour and serve the Lord. Well, Nic's reaction to my grief showed me a lot about the kind of man he was.

The tears flowed freely as I sat on the edge of the back verandah of our homestead and remembered this dear friend who I would not see again until heaven. Nic was not afraid of my tears. He just sat with me. I didn't want words. He didn't speak. his silent presence spoke more than attempted words of comfort could ever have. Although I was grieving the loss of a good friend, I was so grateful that the Lord had brought Nic into my life. Maybe he would have something to do with my future. I would entrust it to the Lord. One day at a time.

So this is how Nic and I became a couple. We spent many days together, and much time on the phone when we couldn't be together. But I hadn't forgotten that I had a goal beyond my new relationship with Nic. I was going back to the land of my heart, back to South Africa. But not before I turned 21! My parents organised a wonderful party on the wide verandahs of our house. Friends from primary school and high school were invited, along with all my cousins and aunties and uncles. Quite a gathering with people coming from all over WA! Even Chris, the guy who'd enthusiastically thanked Nic for my letter, was there with his family. In fact, they provided the entertainment. He and his family played together in a country band. The rain on the evening of the party didn't dampen my spirits. I even had an opportunity to share the gospel during the speeches. I pray the seeds sown then will be watered and one day bear fruit. All the while, Nic helped out and looked on. It was a full-on introduction to my extended family!

FAMILY LIFE

A couple of months after my 21st birthday I was off to South Africa. I had suggested to Nic that if he saw a future for us, he should come with me for a couple of weeks. How could I commit to a person who had not experienced the country which had so pulled at my heart strings? If he couldn't abide Africa, I couldn't remain with him. Drastic you think? Maybe, but that was the extent of the call of the Lord in my life to have some sort of impact in that vast, beautiful, tragic and tumultuous land which was South Africa. Thankfully Nic enjoyed the people, sights and sounds of Africa. Not to the same extent as I did, but enough to satisfy me that if he was willing to wait back home for me, I would come back to him. Parting in South Africa was difficult, maybe even more so for Nic than myself. I had some exciting work to look forward to in an Indian church in Durban whereas Nic had only to go home alone to the routine of his work life. He wept as we said goodbye. It was then that I realised, possibly for the first time, just how much he really cared for me. Although I had no awareness of it at the time, the next few months would test me in ways I could never have expected.

Nic and I had stayed for a little while with the du Plessis family while we were in South Africa together. Since I had visited them when I was on the Doulos, they had moved to a university town called Potchefstroom, about 200km from Johannesburg. It was several hundred kilometres from the coast and bitterly cold in the winter when we were there. Soon after I saw Nic off at the airport, I had to say goodbye to the du Plessis' too. At least they were still in the same country as me! I travelled to Durban feeling both down and excited. I knew I would miss Nic and all my family back home so much, but I was looking forward to all the Lord had in store for me while I was here. The idea was to stay for six months or more, but the details of what I would be doing were pretty sketchy. Who would have thought it would turn so pear-shaped in such a short time? Certainly not me.

Yet belly up it went! At first it was all fine. I was serving in a church which I had spent time in with a team from the Doulos. They were an Indian Baptist seemingly-evangelical church who wanted to challenge their youth to grow and mature in their faith and witness. Along with me, there was a young white man who'd come from outside Durban to work in the same church, but we didn't work together, so we really didn't get to know each other very well. I was living with the pastor, his young family, and his parents. They didn't pay me for the work I did, but they did provide my accommodation and food. I had my own reserves for extra expenses that came my way. The elders of the church were kind and generous and were looking forward to what they hoped would come of our partnership in the ministry. Unfortunately, I would soon find out that the pastor himself, although physically tall and well built, was a weak, manipulative man who was ready to prey on the naivety and vulnerabilities of a young girl who was a long way from home.

Oh, it's not what you might be thinking. He didn't touch me physically, but the emotional manipulation was debilitating. Without going into detail, I was embezzled out of a large sum of money and had the phone in the house cut off to international calls, even though I covered the cost of those calls. When it came to the money, I had been told by the pastor that there was a great need and that I would be paid back soon. It was suggested that I shouldn't bother to talk with the elders about it, but that I should come to him if I had any concerns. So I did just what he said. That was my naivety at play, but even so, I knew something just wasn't right. I was beginning some evangelism training in the area of drama with some of the youth, but I didn't have a lot of help, so the going was difficult. When the phone was cut off and I had been told not to speak with the elders, I felt trapped. On one of my days off, I caught a bus into the city with the young man who was working in the church. For the first time, we had a long chat. It turned out that his experience was not that different from mine. He wasn't hanging around any longer, and in the state I was in, I knew I couldn't either.

After only about eight weeks, I packed up my things and left the church. I didn't ever see a cent of the money which had been 'borrowed' from me. There was never an acknowledgement of any wrongdoing of any kind by the pastor. On the day I announced my leaving to the congregation, one of the elders approached me. He was upset on my behalf. He sincerely took me by the hand and looked me in the eye. "I'm sorry it didn't work out." He gently uttered, "You know you could have come to me at any time. I would've been happy to help you out." He seemed sad and was certainly very genuine in his manner. I'm thankful for his tender heart and his kind spirit. I wonder if he knew of more problems in the church than even I did.

As I left on the bus my mind was reeling. What was that all about? I was so sure I was following God's lead. How could it all go so wrong? How could I get it so wrong? I was quite broken inside and needed time to heal and find some answers. What happened next lifted my spirit no end. Praise God, he doesn't always provide answers, but his presence never leaves us and he always will provide just what we need at the moment we need it. Not when we think we need it, but when we actually do!

The bus I was on was not headed to Potchefstroom, that would be a few days later, but it was headed for Port Elizabeth. "What on earth was at Port Elizabeth?" you ask. Good question! It so happened that my dearest friend from the Doulos, Cecilia, was still serving with the ministry and had travelled ahead of the ship to co-ordinate with churches for the ship's visit in a couple of months' time. Little did she know that I had spoken with her hosts to arrange for a visit. I had asked that it be a surprise for Cecilia and they had wholeheartedly agreed! Graciously they came to the bus depot and picked me up. They seemed as excited to see how Cecilia would react as I was. Well, neither of us expected the reaction we got. When I walked through the door Cecilia let out a blood curdling scream, grabbed me by the arm dragging me into the room and slammed the door! I heard laughter from the other side of the door as she continued squealing and hugging me tightly. What a blessing to be in her presence. The love and acceptance was palpable, such a contrast to the controlling manipulative atmosphere of the place I had just left!

Those few days with Cecilia were healing and refreshing. It would take time to be totally restored in my heart and mind, but I was set on the right path and to this day I'm grateful to God that Cecilia was in South Africa and that I could spend time with her. She truly was and still is a true 'kindred spirit', to quote Anne of Green Gables!

After spending time with Cecilia and her hosts in Port Elizabeth, I was off to the du Plessis' again. The time spent with them before heading home to Australia would bring more healing to my wounded soul. For a few weeks they built me up with words of encouragement, love and acceptance. I know that as Christians we often call other Christians, brothers and sisters, and rightly so. Through Christ we are brothers and sisters if we profess faith in Him. But with the du Plessis', the terms 'brother' and 'sister' were not just words. They were a reality. As I thank the Lord for Cecilia, I also give Him thanks for the dear friends I have in Elaine and Louis. God willing, I will again meet all of these dear people before I'm called to my eternal home in heaven. But if not, I will look forward to celebrating with them there for an eternity.

Chapter 6

To Say 'I Do' or Not to Say 'I Do'!

Finally, I had a journey home which was straight forward. No trouble at airports, no concerns with passports or tickets, no need for directions from strangers. I had a lot of time to think; most of my thoughts were of Nic. Now my head was turned for home, what was the future for Nic and I? Looking back, I can see that my parents were a bit put out. I had had the best and the worst of times in South Africa, but when they came to get me at the airport at some unearthly hour of the night, it was Nic who dominated my space. After all they'd done for me, they were now starting to feel a little on the outside. To this day I feel bad about that. I guess at some point my focus in my relationships was going to veer from my parents to my future partner, but it was hard going all the same. I know for a fact that without their encouragement, support and help I couldn't have done any of the things I had done in the previous few years. I hope and pray they have forgiven me my lack of attention to them at this time. To paraphrase a famous scientist, I was only able to go as far as I had, and do as much as I did because I was standing on their shoulders. I know that wherever life leads, I have a home with them.

Then there was Nic. For now, my time in South Africa was over. I hoped I would one day go back there again, but next time maybe I would take my family along with me. Hang on a minute! I was single; I didn't have a family to take with me! Not yet anyway. Nic and I were now deeply committed to each other and our love for one another was growing every day. The next logical step was for us to marry. If not, then we should break up. We couldn't just stay boyfriend and girlfriend. We were either husband and wife, or we were nothing. But what if he wasn't the right one? I was hoping the Lord would make it as clear to me as he had regarding my joining the Doulos. I prayed every day for clear direction from Him, but it seemed every time I opened the scriptures, I would read something which was very ambiguous! I was getting nowhere.

Then one evening in Three Springs my uncle was hosting a travelling minister. Dad, Mum and I went to my uncle's house for dinner and a meeting and it was all quite lovely. Nothing ground-shaking, but lovely all the same. After the man had finished speaking, he asked if anyone wanted prayer for anything. Of course I did, but I didn't ask for it. I'd really had enough ambiguous answers to my prayers. I'm sure that there were others who needed this man to pray for them much more than I did! God had other thoughts! He prayed for this and that person and then he came over to me. He put his hand on my shoulder and started to speak to me. his voice was gentle, yet firm and clear. This is the gist of what he said to me: "I believe you have a big decision to make. I feel that the Lord wants you to know that because of your heart to love and serve Him, he will bless whatever you choose." Well, I didn't know this man from a bar of soap, but I sure was facing a very big decision! That wasn't really what I had wanted to hear, however. A 'God wants you to marry the man you're asking about' would have been nice, or a 'Run for your life, he's not for you' would have been acceptable too. But 'You choose'? That wasn't what I was looking for, I didn't even ask to be prayed for by this travelling preacher man!

With all this going through my mind I felt a strong rebuke from the Lord. Over the next few days I felt the Lord speak to me very clearly. He showed me through the scriptures that I wasn't a child in my faith anymore. He'd given me enough milk and I was ready for the meat. Where he had to lead me before, like a mother holding the hand of her tiny, tottering toddler, making sure I knew each step would be firm before placing my foot down, now he was letting me go. He had taught me that his will for my life was contained within his word. As long as I didn't overstep the boundaries the Word set out, I was in his will. He was treating me like a grown up. I remember being quite dumbfounded at the idea. I was not a babe in his arms anymore, but a fellow worker with and for Christ. As Jesus gave instructions to his disciples, then sent them out, his word had all the instructions I needed to make the decisions which would be pleasing to Him. The key was in the words of the preacher, "because of your heart to love and serve the Lord, whatever you choose, he will bless."

Oh, he was so right. All along, my desire was to be pleasing to the Lord. I lost count of how many times I muffed it, but that desire remained the same come what may. That was why I wanted to know if Nic was the right one or not. I wanted desperately to please my Lord. Now the Lord was telling me that because I desperately wanted to please him, my choices would be ok. I still find that amazing. God would trust me. I didn't even trust me a lot of the time, yet he did. I love him so much, but I don't ever think I could love him as much as he loves me. I was certainly going to give it my best shot, for the rest of my life.

'That's all good and well', I can hear your thoughts, 'but where does that leave Nic? What did you choose?'. I'll put you out of your misery, if you haven't guessed already, I chose Nic! With the approval of my parents, we decided to marry and thought a long engagement unnecessary. All we needed was enough time to prepare for the wedding, four months should do it. We would marry on the back verandah of the homestead at Wanneranooka. Nothing too fancy, but it would be just perfect. My sisters would be my bridesmaids and Nic's brother and best mate would be his groomsmen. I asked Cecilia if she would be a bridesmaid too, but she wasn't able to make it to Australia. I would have Dad and Mum walk me up the aisle to Nic, and everyone in attendance could sit on hay bales covered in calico fabric under the open sky while the ceremony took place with the bridal party under the verandah. What could go wrong? Well, since it was July, there might be rain. No, I was sure the weather would be just fine!

But the weather didn't turn out to be fine. Not at first anyway. My sister's boyfriend Geoff, who was a Baptist minister at the time, was going to give the sermon at the wedding. As he was staying at the farm, he was there nice and early to see the gentle rain set in. The hay bale seats were covered in black plastic so people wouldn't get wet back-sides, but not much else could be done. I remember at one point hearing him declare "I've been walking around praying for a while now and I think it's the most faithless prayer I've ever prayed. I just don't think this rain is going to stop!" How wrong he was. By the time the wedding commenced, the plastic was off the bales and the air was dry. It was bitterly cold, but at least it was dry! It turned out to be a beautiful day. The skies did open up again, but by that time we were at the reception in the town hall, so it could rain as much as it liked then!

It's a strange feeling saying goodbye to the guests at your own wedding. All the work, time and effort that so many people put in, had paid off. In my eyes, it went beautifully. Not without its hitches, but it was a beautiful day for me. Chris Sorahan, the AOG pastor, officiated at the ceremony, my sister's boyfriend (and future husband), gave the sermon, my sister Kathryn made the cake and her husband Darren was the MC at the reception. Not to mention the countless hours Mum and Dad put in behind the scenes to make the day so special. There was still so much cleaning up and packing away to do, but Nic and I were off. No longer Jennifer Haeusler, but Jennifer de Vries. In my heart, I think I'll always feel like a Haeusler, but my life now was moving forward as a de Vries, the wife of my much loved and chosen man Nic. It was the end of a chapter of my life and the beginning of a new one. Only the Lord knew what the future held for Nic and I. As we waved goodbye and drove away from the town hall, my heart was filled with hope, but only God knew.

It's just as well that I didn't know what I had signed up for, as the first year of marriage was extremely difficult for me. Not because of Nic, he was wonderful and worked very hard for us as a fledgling family. But he was a shift worker remember, so for four days a week I didn't see much of him at all. To top that off, I didn't feel at all at home at the church we were attending, and I began to feel very lonely. Although Chris, who officiated at our wedding, and his wife Marion and family were very good to us, I didn't really feel like I fitted in at church. You know that awful feeling you get when you're kind of on the 'outer' of a group. That's how I felt. Not the church's fault, I just think the Lord wanted us somewhere else, so I really couldn't settle down. Funnily enough, Nic seemed to feel the same, so after much discussion we decided that we would look for a church family where we would feel more at home together. We wanted to keep some sort of continuity in our fellowship, so we agreed that we would visit a different church every second week, while attending our usual church the other week. In this way we could still stay regularly connected with one church family. It turned out to be a good decision and soon enough we found a place to call home; a place where we would make many dear friends and would have opportunities to serve the Lord. Life was still not always easy, but we were making headway!

It didn't take long for us to settle in at Geraldton Baptist Church. As I didn't have a job, I was able to help out with some of the admin and get involved in various ministries. My favourite was serving with the pastor in Prison Fellowship. In fact, as I had time during the week, I also visited the prison during the week with a pastor and co-worker from another church. It was uncanny how often I would feel unwell on the days that I was going out to the prison. Many times I didn't feel like it, but remembering how much the prisoners needed to know the life-changing message of the gospel would be motivation enough to drag myself out there. Almost every time I did, the headache, stomach ache or whatever ailment I had been feeling, would go away and we would have a wonderful time sharing of the love of Christ with the prisoners who attended. I would come away feeling blessed, even though my goal was to be a blessing. Isn't that just how the Lord often works? If our motivation is the encouragement of others, we so often feel encouraged in turn. Is that the law of sowing and reaping? Maybe. I may not have been in Africa, but I could still be a part of bringing the good news of the gospel to those who really needed it but who were much closer to home.

It seemed I had a new direction in life. I had a husband who I loved deeply and who loved me. I had a church family who welcomed me and nurtured me in my faith and witness and whom I could serve in many ways. I was involved in a ministry which I was sure would bring lasting hope to many. Yes, I felt like I could do this for a while. I had forgotten that many years ago I had asked the Lord to always direct my steps. Sometimes he spoke clearly, sometimes he gently encouraged me, sometimes he allowed things to happen to me, sometimes he gave me the choice, but all the while he was surely and certainly at the helm steering my life to where he wanted me to go. God was about to make sure I didn't feel settled for too long though. If he'd left me to go the way I felt the most comfortable with, maybe I would have stopped trusting so much in Him and started relying on my own abilities. No, when I gave my life to Christ, he took me seriously and he was about to lead me on yet another path. I didn't think I was quite ready for this new direction, but he knew me better than I knew myself and I will always be grateful that he was and is in control.

CHAPTER 7

IN THE FAMILY WAY

If you haven't worked it out yet, the new direction the Lord was leading me to was parenting! Yes, one year and three months after Nic and I were married I fell pregnant. In fact, the due date of our first baby was our second wedding anniversary, the 13th of July! As we hadn't exactly been planning on having children for another 6 months or so, the news was a shock. As I have previously mentioned, things were ticking along quite nicely thank you. Now I would have to get used to a new normal; again! I'll never forget Nic's reaction when I told him we were expecting our first child. his eyes softened in wonder, almost to the point of tears. He was sitting on the sofa in the lounge room of our rented house as I sat down next to him. He reached over and placed his warm hand on my abdomen, as if to welcome our little one into his life and his heart. I would have only been about six weeks pregnant at this stage. It was the strangest feeling, to know that a new life was being formed inside me, yet at this point I didn't feel any different than I had before. Not physically anyway, emotionally was a different story. Happy, nervous, concerned. I was a Mum. Nic was a Dad. We'd not yet met our precious little one, but he was already welcomed into our family.

After forty weeks and three days, our precious baby boy was born. Although the pregnancy had been pretty straight forward, the birth was not at all. My poor body didn't seem to know what was going on! Oh, I'd read books; I knew how it was all going to work. I'd prayed over every aspect of the birth and expected nothing but a joyful, relatively pain-free experience. Huh! A challenging lesson was brewing! A test of endurance. An epic trial! Firstly, my labour continued for 25 hours, although even that was hard to calculate as the contractions were never regular, being anywhere from one minute to three minutes or more apart right up to delivery! Then there was the pain relief. Oh yes, I wasn't spared pain! When the nurse gave me pethidine for it, I promptly vomited all over the place. She'd neglected to inform me that it could make me nauseous. Hmmm, I figured that one out soon enough. Then came the delivery itself. I was exhausted after 24 hours with nothing going the way I had hoped. I had to have my waters broken and I even had to have an episiotomy. For the uninitiated, that means they took a large pair of surgical scissors and cut me so my baby could be more easily delivered. It makes me shudder to remember and I can still hear the crunching sound even now. According to the doctor, the reason I was having trouble getting my little one out was because I was just too tired and didn't have the energy. I'd go along with that! Finally, at 9:05 in the morning on the 15th of July 1998 our precious Samuel was born; praise the Lord for a perfect little boy!

I've heard it said that to have a hard labour is to have an easy baby! Well, I think that's an old wives' tale, but in my case it was certainly true. Samuel was a model baby. We worked on getting him into a feed, wake and sleep routine. Fortunately, he fed well, slept well and was generally a very contented baby. At five weeks of age he even slept through the night. What was everyone going on about? This parenting was easy! I learnt later that not all babies were like this. Feeding and sleep times were not always so straight forward; but at least I had a great start to my parenting journey with Samuel. In fact, we figured that since we'd begun having children we might as well continue. A two-year gap sounded like a good idea, so that's how we planned it. I was soon to learn, however, that although I fell pregnant easily, it wasn't always so easy to stay that way.

When Samuel was about 16 months old, we were thrilled to discover that we were in the family way again. That would make his new sibling exactly two years younger. How could we have planned it better? That is until a few weeks later when I started to bleed. No, this is not right. My heart was racing as we visited the doctor who examined me and gave me an ultrasound. My fears were realised when she gently informed us that I had miscarried and that the baby was no more. I'd never felt such grief. We'd only known that I was pregnant for a few weeks, yet already we had welcomed this little one into our hearts and lives, just as we had Samuel when he was being formed in the womb. We already had hopes and dreams for our child, yet now, suddenly, it was all over. At six weeks I wept over the loss of what would have been. I couldn't believe that this would happen to me. Surely this only happened to other people. Not to me. Not to my family.

I felt like my heart was broken into a thousand tiny pieces. The sorrow was so deep. The pain tangible. I remember sitting outside one evening staring up at the stars and crying out to the Lord, 'I don't expect an answer, but I just have to ask the question: Why? Why did this have to happen to me?' I didn't ever get an answer. I didn't really even want one. It wouldn't have helped. I just had to ask the question and get it off my chest. Although the voice of the Father was barely audible as my soul grieved, his quiet presence was very real. It seemed his ever loving and understanding spirit whispered to mine, "I know the pain of losing a child. I am with you always." It was enough. Eventually I came to have peace in my heart. I would see my little one someday. When I reach heaven, he or she will be waiting for me, and we will be able to spend an eternity together in the presence of our Lord. What a joyous hope I have as I wait for that day.

It was again with mixed feelings that we found we were expecting only about six weeks after I had miscarried. I was apprehensive that I might lose this precious little one as well. I prayed and tried to trust wholeheartedly in the Lord, but I must admit, I didn't really relax into the pregnancy until I was past the six-week mark. Somehow I felt that our new baby was safe then. Praise the Lord he was. Although it was a very emotionally difficult pregnancy, messing with my head in many ways, the labour was wonderful. My body had finally figured out how this labour thing worked and although he was ten days overdue, Mitchell arrived after only an eight-hour labour; another beautiful baby boy. We had so much to be thankful for. Our two boys were truly a blessing from the Lord, certainly no mixed emotion there!

I will never cease to be amazed at the awesome work of the Lord. How the same two people can have two children who are so completely different! That was Samuel and Mitchell. I had been used to a very placid yet vocal baby in Samuel, now I had a very active yet quiet one in Mitchell! It sounds like a contradiction, but it really wasn't. Let me explain. He wasn't at all fussy, but he was very wriggly! Even in the womb I noticed he liked to push out on his feet - very uncomfortable! At only five months of age he pulled himself onto his feet. Soon after we found him holding onto the rails of his cot bouncing with all his might and sporting a huge grin on his face! He wasn't much of a talker, but you could see in his eyes that there was a lot going on inside that little mind. He went on be a climber; beds, chairs, ladders, trees, wooden pallets and almost anything that could be climbed. What a surprising wonder, we now had a busy thinker on our hands!

Life was very full with two little boys to run around after. They were no trouble at all, besides the fact that Samuel never stopped talking and Mitchell never stopped climbing things! I think I had it pretty easy really.

That is until a series of devastating events which shook my little family's world. In a period of just three months, my faith would be stretched almost to its limit. I was to find out how far-reaching the hand of the Lord was and how much his presence goes behind and before in all life's circumstances, both good and bad.

It began like this. We were travelling back to Geraldton after attending a friend's wedding some 800km away. The sun was setting as we took to the road for the final leg of the journey. It was a bad time of the day to be driving through the bush. The wildlife often would come out to feed on the roadside at dusk and there was always a risk that one would venture onto the road. In all our trips to Perth and beyond we'd avoided any collisions; this time was to be different. The boys were in their car seats and settling down to sleep when a kangaroo hopped out onto the middle of the road. There was nothing we could do but plough right on into it. Seeing such a beautiful creature killed in such a gruesome way was not something I coped with very well. On top of the fact that I was extremely tired it was all a bit much. I couldn't keep my emotion under control as I tried to comfort the boys who were now very much awake. The kangaroo was very dead and the front end of our car had suffered significant damage. Praise God we were all ok. But just the same, the event had shaken me considerably.

A couple of weeks later, we received a phone call that Nic's dad had collapsed at home and had been rushed into hospital with a suspected heart attack. The days that followed were tense and intense as we waited to find out exactly what was going on and if he would be ok. His condition was serious, but fortunately could be managed with medication and a change in diet. We had opportunity to give thanks to God for the gradual physical restoration of my father-in-law.

A reprieve from our troubles came a few weeks later at Christmas time when we came together at Wanneranooka with my parents and sisters and their husbands and children. It was to be the last Christmas on the farm before it was sold so it was a very special time for all of us. Both my sisters were expecting, and during the short time we were all together, I took a pregnancy test and discovered that I too was to be a Mum again! All three of us together and pregnant at the same time. Now that was something worth celebrating! Christmas that year will be remembered fondly by all of us for as long as we live. It had been such a special time of reminiscing of the past and looking forward with hope to the future. Unfortunately the joy of our last time together on the family farm would be overshadowed for Nic and I by the trials that were still to come.

A month or so after the trauma of Nic's dad's health scare came that fateful day which I will never forget. By now we had moved out of our rented house and were living in a shed which Nic had built on a property he'd purchased before we met. It was a comfortable shed, so certainly no complaints there, but our new house was being built just a few metres away. The boys didn't mind living on a construction site. It meant having big piles of dirt to play in and seeing machinery come and go. They also loved chatting with the brickies who were working on our house. On one particular day, however, Mitchell was outside playing around the house when I heard a blood curdling scream. Now Mitchell was a tough little nut, so to hear him scream like that made a chill run down my spine. I dropped whatever I was doing and bolted outside to find him.

My little 18-month-old toddler who loved to climb things had climbed up a jarrah timber pallet left leaning against the wall of the house. Somehow the pallet had fallen over with Mitchell hanging on and had landed on top of him. When I found him, all I could see was the top of his head sticking out and his little body being crushed by the weight of the pallet. Immediately I lifted the pallet off and picked him up. his screaming didn't decrease but only intensified. The moment I'd picked him up, his nose began to bleed and I noticed it was sitting at a very strange angle. By now Nic had joined us. I remember telling him I thought Mitchell had broken his nose and that we needed to take him to the hospital. While we carefully placed him in the car Nic suggested I stay home with Samuel while he call ahead and then drive Mitchell to the emergency department. I couldn't stand the thought of staying at home while one of my precious little ones was whisked off to the hospital so I adamantly put a bewildered Samuel in his car seat and clambered in the middle, squeezing between the car seats so I could monitor Mitchell as Nic drove.

As he always does, the Lord was leading me that day, even though at the time I felt like I was only reacting to what was going on around me. On the way to the hospital, Mitchell fell unconscious. Any first aid training I'd completed came back to me. I was going over and over in my mind what I would do if he stopped breathing or started convulsing or any other such scenario. He came to, but soon passed out again. By the time we reached the hospital the staff were ready and waiting for us. Mitchell was swiftly taken into emergency and we hurriedly followed, all three of us, Nic, Samuel and myself. The doctor examined Mitchell and informed us that the nose would be fine. They're pretty flexible at that age apparently. But there were still a lot of concerns. A bent nose would not cause a child to fall unconscious. Mitchell at this time was lucid, but whenever he was laid down, he would scream the same scream I'd heard when he'd initially fallen. The doctor wanted to investigate further so he led us down the passage to the x-ray room; he wanted to take a look at Mitchell's skull.

To this day I don't know how they were able to keep Mitchell still enough to get those x-rays. Every time they lay him down on the stretcher he would scream in pain. As I was pregnant, I could only stand outside the room and listen in. How I wanted to rush and hold my little boy and let him know that it was all going to be ok. But was it? My head was telling me that anything could happen, yet in my heart there was a surreal peace. I knew God was at work. The result of the x-ray confirmed what the doctor had thought. Mitchell had a fracture in his skull which went from the centre at the top, down the middle at the back, then separated in two different directions like an upside-down Y. A fractured skull! What did that mean for Mitchell? I didn't know. How could I? I wasn't a doctor.

Even the doctors weren't sure what to do. First, they called the children's hospital in Perth to confer, then they called the flying doctor to give them notice that they may be needed to fly a patient to Perth, then they conferred with specialists in Perth again. The dilemma was such that they needed to do a CAT scan of Mitchell's head, but the situation for that to occur was less than ideal. For starters, they suspected that there was bleeding on the brain, in which case the changing air pressure in an aeroplane would be detrimental to Mitchell. On the other hand, if there was bleeding on the brain, Mitchell would definitely need to be in Perth anyway; so what should they do?

Well, they came to the conclusion that the best thing to do was to perform the scan in Geraldton, and after getting the results they would make a further decision about a course of action. With that in mind, Nic went home to get a change of clothes for Mitchell and myself and to sort Samuel out, (some friends had come earlier and collected him from the hospital for us when we realised we would be there awhile). A few minutes after Nic left, however, a doctor came to me and said that since the flying doctor was ready for us we might as well fly to Perth now and the scan could be done down there. Oh no! Nic had just gone home! We couldn't leave without letting him know what was going on and there was no way we could contact him at this point. I explained this the best I could to the doctor, and he made the decision right there that we would not go to Perth, but that we would just go ahead with the scan as was the original plan. I was grateful for his understanding. Looking back I can see that the Lord placed just the right doctor for Mitchell and for us in the emergency department that day. In every way he encouraged and supported us, all the while tending to Mitchell and his needs.

For the doctor's wonderful manner and consideration I will be forever grateful, especially through the next few hours. For Mitchell to undergo a CAT scan he had to be perfectly still. As was very clear to all of us he would have to be sedated for this to happen. Unfortunately, however, sedating a young child with a head injury was not so straight forward. First a drip had to be inserted into the back of his hand. It took two nurses and myself to hold an 18-month-old down to get the needle in. How my heart ached for my little one. He didn't understand that it was for his good. All he knew was that he was in incredible pain, and I was making it worse. After much thrashing around and screaming the drip was finally in and the doctor was able to begin administration of the sedative. He informed me that it was a tricky situation. He had to get the dose just right. Too much to a child with a head injury and he could slow Mitchell's heart down to a stop; that wouldn't be good! Too little and he would not be still for the scan which would make the whole exercise futile. Little by little he administered the drug through the drip. I watched as my little boy slowly succumbed. It was unnerving to see him lying limp on the stretcher, but thankfully the doctor had got it just right.

Mitchell was all hooked up to monitors so they could see that his heart didn't slow too much and we were ready to go. Again, the doctor spoke to my heart as he asked me to sit on the stretcher with my unconscious child while he was being wheeled to the room where the scan would take place. "You sit with him until the last minute," he encouraged me, "I'll let you know when to leave the room. As soon as the scan is over I want you to come back and sit with him again." Oh what a blessing. It was all quite surreal as we were being wheeled down the long and unfamiliar corridors. My head was a mess, yet somehow in my spirit, I knew everything would be ok. A scripture came to my mind which I had committed to memory in my teenage years: " "For I know the plans I have for you" declares the Lord, "plans to prosper you and not to harm you, to give you a hope and a future"" (Jeremiah 29:11). At that moment I sensed a deep peace. This was God's word for Mitchell. He wasn't going to die. God had a plan. He had a future. As we rolled down the quiet corridors, my head still grappled with the situation, but my spirit was at rest.

Then came the most incredible news. The scan was completed and we were back in recovery. Mitchell was still under the influence of the sedative and would have to stay in overnight to be monitored, but the look of wonder on the doctor's face as he gave us the results of the scan was clear. "There is no bleeding on the brain. Mitchell's brain is just fine! You have a very lucky boy there." My spirit soared, and this time my head caught up! It wasn't luck which preserved my son's brain, it was God. He had a plan and a future in store for Mitchell, and no jarrah pallet was about to prevent that future from unfolding. To say the least, Nic and I were relieved. How could we do anything but praise the Lord. It was suggested that I go home and get a good night's sleep while the next doctor on shift monitored Mitchell through the night. They had to be kidding right? I wasn't about to leave my boy now! Nic again went home to fetch some more things and to look after Samuel while I settled on the lounge in Mitchell's recovery room. What a day it had been. The worst of it was over, just the last leg of our time at hospital to see through. I was only just beginning to see what an amazing God I served, but he hadn't finished teaching me about his care and protection yet.

The next morning Mitchell woke up and though he was still a bit wobbly on his feet, he already was trying to climb out of the hospital cot, not a good idea when the cot had bars over the top! The last thing I wanted him to do was bump his head again. As all his ob's had been satisfactory overnight, Mitchell was discharged in the morning. We were sent home with strict instructions to make sure Mitchell didn't bump his head, especially at the back where the fracture in the skull diverged in two directions. Oh sure! That would be easy. Mitchell was just a passive little thing. NOT! For the next 6 weeks, my task was clear. Make sure Mitchell didn't bump his head. After that, the fracture would have healed and all would be well. I stuck close by him whatever he was doing. He was never out of my sight. I had to keep him safe. It was all up to me. But was it? The Lord was going to wake me up to the fact in a very clear and heart-wrenching way that my children were first his, then mine and that ultimately He was their protector, not me.

The day had started in the most usual of ways. Everything was just fine as the boys and I sat at the table for a meal. I think Nic was at work, so the duty of watching out for Mitchell was mine alone. Well, that's what I thought! As we sat at the table, out of the blue, Mitchell fell off his chair backwards. What? He had the best balance of any toddler I'd ever met, why would he do that? My heart must have stopped beating as it all seemed to occur in slow motion. Mitchell landed hard on the concrete floor. Have you ever seen a child fall backwards off a chair? Their back hits the floor then their head squarely follows suit. But not this time. As Mitchell's back hit the floor, his head stayed up. It was as if an invisible hand was holding it off the hard cold concrete. Immediately I broke out in goose bumps all over. Although I had not heard quite this clearly for a while, the Lord spoke directly to my heart and mind, "You are doing all you can to protect your child, but he is my child and I am the one who is really protecting him!" Emotion rose in my throat as I realised that I had left God out of the picture. I had taken on Mitchell's recovery as though I was on my own. I repented then and there. I would still look out for Mitchell, Samuel and any other children God would bless us with, but my focus needed to be on him, not on me. I wondered too, if it was actually an angel who had pushed Mitchell off that chair, then nursed his head on the way down. I will never know, this side of heaven, but I do know that I will never forget the lesson I was taught that day.

You'd think that after the collision with the kangaroo, Nic's Dad's health scare and Mitchell's accident that things might have returned to normal for a while. Unfortunately our troubles weren't over yet. On the horizon another devastating event was about to occur.

It had only been a couple of weeks since Mitchell had recovered when I started to bleed again. Not again! In some ways I almost expected it. I hadn't felt the usual things you feel in the early weeks of pregnancy, but since every pregnancy is different, I hadn't paid it too much attention. Now of course I did. Nic and I were able to get an appointment that day to see a doctor, so we found a sitter to watch Samuel and Mitchell. I had to hold my emotion back as we nervously waited in the surgery for the doctor to call us in. He listened as I explained what was happening then he sent me off to have an ultrasound. We silently drove the few kilometres to the hospital for the scan. Anxiously we watched the screen for any signs of life we could find. I was about ten weeks pregnant at this stage. We should have been able to hear a heartbeat and see some movement. My womb was silent and motionless. The radiographer who performed the ultrasound gently and with great compassion informed us that we had lost our baby. She offered us tissues and gave us time alone together to process the heart-breaking news.

After taking some time, holding each other tight and crying it out, Nic and I had to return to the doctor for a more complete diagnosis and a 'treatment' plan. To our further dismay, we couldn't see our usual doctor,

IN THE FAMILY WAY

but another who we didn't know very well. He was cold and impersonal, choosing to stare at his computer screen as he explained exactly what had happened. "You have had a blighted ovum," he blandly announced. "It has been reabsorbed into your body". What the heck did that mean?! "Was I actually pregnant then?" My words were veiled behind a thin veneer of control. "Oh yes, you were definitely pregnant, sometimes though when things are not well with the fertilised ovum this can happen. The womb prepares for the baby, the placenta forms, but the ovum is not viable and is reabsorbed." I don't remember him looking us in the eyes at all. I don't even remember him looking away from the computer screen. "I can book you in for a D and C today." Emotion rose again in me at his suggestion that I should endure a dilation and curette. I didn't want some stranger scraping me out. What if they were wrong? What if there was a chance that my little one was still there, hiding beyond the scan's waves? No, I had to speak up.

I spoke firmly even though my voice was quavering as I asked, "Can I allow things to happen naturally? I'd rather not have medical intervention if I don't need to." Nic supported me all the way. This was too much for us to process. Our baby was gone somehow, yet my womb had continued to develop to support the life that was never to be. We just couldn't understand what was going on. The doctor was surprised at our response, but he informed us that I didn't have to have a D and C if I didn't want one. I should just go home then and rest until the miscarriage was complete. A moment later we found ourselves back in the car driving home. Although emotion was still close to the surface, I was able to hold it in. After all, I had felt that things were a bit strange with this pregnancy. All the same, I'd rather not speak too much about it and just get on with things. I'd miscarried before. I knew what to expect. At least, I thought I did.

It was late afternoon when Nic and I got home. I suppose we tried to continue as normally as we could. He would have bathed the boys and got them ready for bed and I would have got the dinner ready. Samuel and Mitchell were unaware of all the hardships Nic and I were facing at this moment. They didn't need to know. How could we explain it to them anyway? In a few days it would all be over and we could think about what to do next. I slept restlessly that night, hoping beyond hope that the doctor and the radiologist were wrong and that everything would work out fine. I prayed and placed my family in the Lord's hands. May his will be done. Nic slept soundly as was usual for him, but for me sleep didn't come easily.

The next morning felt a little strange as we sat up for breakfast together, yesterday was gone with its emotion and turmoil and a new day was beginning. Praise God that Nic was on his rostered days off. Little did I know at the time, but I was really going to need his firm and loving care this day. As we ate together my womb started to cramp. Period pain! Great, that's all I need. I told Nic that I was going to stand under a hot shower and see if that helped at all. Oblivious to what was about to occur Nic continued breakfasting with the boys as I proceeded to the shower. The hot water didn't help. The cramping became more and more intense as pain radiated from my womb. Doubled over I pressed my hands against my abdomen trying to stem the pain. It didn't work. What was this feeling? I felt I needed to push! At this point my body took over. As if in labour, my womb contracted painfully and I bore down hard. What happened next shocked me to a point nigh on hysteria.

Suddenly I felt a pop and there was a rush of blood from my contracting womb. More than that; Oh Lord help me, there was a mass the size of a grapefruit which was expelled from my body. My heart grew faint as in anguish and fright I cried out, "Nic, Nic, Nic ....." My tone didn't leave Nic wondering if I was serious. He hurriedly left the table and came to me. I can only imagine what went through his mind as he saw me barely standing and sobbing with blood and tissue mass all over the floor of the shower.

The seriousness of the situation struck home and Nic went decisively into action. He quickly turned the shower off and covered me in a towel before attending to the boys and directing them to their bedroom. He locked the door not wanting them to be exposed to what was unfolding in the bathroom. No sooner than he'd left and he was back. He helped me get dry and dressed and settled me down on the sofa in our lounge room. As I lay there in a state of shock still crying and shaking, he went back to the bathroom to clean up the shower and deal with what turned out to be the sack and the life support for our baby that never was to be, the placenta, that had been expelled from my womb.

I am so grateful that the Lord gave me a husband who is calm in an emergency. In my grief I couldn't think straight, but Nic had the clarity of mind to find some pretty wrapping paper and wrap up the sodden mass from the shower floor. He held his emotion together and asked me what I wanted to do with it. I didn't know what to do. What was I supposed to do? I just couldn't work it out. "Just get rid of it." But that wasn't the right thing to do. Nic soon realised that I wasn't in a fit state to make a decision, so he made one on my behalf. He suggested that we have a little ceremony and bury it under the peach tree in our orchard. Okay. That would be good.

Gently Nic led me out to the orchard, I felt weak but secure in the strong arms of my loving husband. I stood still as he dug a hole and placed the precious parcel on the bottom. As he filled it in, his emotion overflowed as did mine. This is all that was left of our little one. It represented another child who we would not have the privilege or joy of knowing until we finally met in heaven. With a broken and soft voice Nic prayed and committed the life that was, to the Lord, along with our family and our future. We stood by the tree in each other's arms and wept. The Lord was with us. As we held each other, he held us. He sustained us. I believe he wept with us. Again, his gentle presence prevailed in the depth of our trials.

As the tears subsided, we slowly and silently walked back to the shed, lost in our thoughts, as ready as we would ever be to face the boys and our day. In the best way we knew how we explained to Samuel and Mitchell what had just happened. I'm not sure what they were able to take in, but their love and hugs were, as always, so very healing to my hurting soul. I was so blessed to have at least two healthy happy children and I was thankful to the Lord for them.

A couple of hours later, Nic decided that he needed to pick something up from the hardware store. He asked me if I'd like him to take the boys along for a ride so I could have some time alone, but that was the last thing I wanted at that moment. I just wanted to forget for a while, so I asked if we could all go together. He compassionately agreed and we clambered into the car. As we wondered around the store I was keenly aware of the fact that life was just going on as usual all around us. People were chatting, shopping, pondering their next purchase, working at the till, and here I was, having just lost my little one. It was good to be around people though. It helped me feel more normal. That is until the moment I had another massive loss of blood. My strength seemed to flow out of me with it. I grabbed Nic's arm, "I have to go to the toilet, I think I'm going to be sick." As quickly as I could I stumbled down the aisles until I reached the public toilets at the front corner of the shop. As I closed the door I collapsed on the floor. I was conscious, but felt just so weak. I sat there for a while hoping my strength would return enough to find Nic. Finally, I rose and as I washed my face I caught a glimpse of myself in the mirror, I knew then I needed to go the hospital, my face was deathly white.

With God's help I managed to find Nic and the boys and he rushed me down to emergency. They didn't make us wait but hurriedly took me in. Praise God, our family doctor was available. Nic stayed with me until the doctor came, then took the boys out for a treat while he saw to me. He had me lie down in a quiet room and did some tests. The large loss of blood I'd experienced at the hardware store seemed to be the last of it, but the doctor ordered me to rest for an hour or so in the hospital anyway. In the meantime, he asked me if I'd had an anti-D injection. I responded in the negative. I knew that since I had a negative blood type I needed to have the injection after giving birth, but I didn't know I needed it after miscarriage! Again, I can only give thanks to the Lord that I ended up in the hospital that afternoon. If I hadn't, I would've had the anti-D injection too late. If I didn't have the injection within forty-eight hours, my body would reject any future babies growing in my womb unless they also had a negative blood type. Through the trauma which was that day, I was able to see the goodness of my Lord, in the compassion, understanding, kindness and professionalism of our family doctor, in the loving and consistent care of my husband, in the sparkly eyes, hearty laughs and warm hugs of our boys. I was going to be okay; my Lord would not let me go.

In the months that followed I held on tight to God. Each new day meant another tiny piece of my wounded heart was made well. Although for years I would remember and feel the sorrow and pain of our loss, by God's grace I could keep moving forward. Samuel and Mitchell were growing fast and were a constant source of blessing to Nic and I. We loved them so much, but felt that our family was not yet complete. It took me awhile to feel like I was ready to conceive again, but after several months, that's just what I did! If I was nervous after my first miscarriage, I was triply so after my second! For a long time I didn't want to even hope for the future of this baby. If I lost this one too, my hopes wouldn't be realised for the third time. Hallelujah! I had nothing to worry about.

My pregnancy went off without a hitch and on the 12th of January, after twelve hours of hard labour, I gave birth to a strong and healthy boy. We named him Justin Caleb, a strong name which means 'upright and wholehearted'. He was a precious and easy-going baby. Only ten days after he was born he started sleeping through the night! What a wonderful thing to have another baby in our home again. He was very placid and content to sit and watch the world go by. As he grew he developed a love for books. On his second birthday he was given a series of small board books by my sister and her family. His reaction was priceless: "Books, books, books!" he squealed with delight. And that's just what he was, a delight. Quite a quirky little thing he was too. As he was so content watching the world go by and looking at the books and playing with the toys around him, he didn't seem to feel the need to move around! It wasn't until about 5 months of age that he decided to sit up (this was the age Mitchell started to stand up and walk along holding onto things!). He didn't ever crawl either but instead just shuffled along on his bottom while sitting upright. This all made life much easier for me. For such a long time I could plonk him down on a rug with some books and toys and know that he wouldn't move from that spot until I came back and picked him up. The Lord knew I needed to have a reprieve from the trouble of the year before.

By the time Justin turned two, I was in the family way again by eight months. I had been concerned about this pregnancy as much as the others. In my weird logic I thought that I had a good chance of miscarrying again. My history had been: baby, miscarriage, baby, miscarriage, baby .... The pattern suggested I would miscarry. Crazy I know, maybe it was the hormones, but needless to say, I treasured every movement I felt of my growing baby - every hiccup, every kick - just in case it was all I would know of my child.

It was with great relief that our fourth and final biological baby, Darcy Wentworth, was born on the 15th of February 2005. It was a difficult yet exhilarating birth. Before we had any children, I'd hoped that I could give birth without any intervention. For Samuel, Mitchell and Justin I had something or other to help me along, mostly just the gas to help relieve pain. But with Darcy, I was able to do it without anything but the encouragement of my wonderful husband and a sympathetic midwife. Even though Darcy's position was posterior (his spine to my spine), which made for a drawn-out labour with severe back ache, he didn't need any assistance to emerge. Even this God had in hand. We didn't know how he was positioned in the womb until his head was delivered, but after he was born the midwife commented that I couldn't have been in a better position for delivering a posterior baby. We praised God again for a healthy strong baby and for the blessing of our beautiful and wonderful sons Samuel, Mitchell, Justin and now Darcy.

Well, it was the end of the journey of childbirth for me. No more children would be born to Nic and I. I felt a sadness that my womb would never be the home for a new life again, yet somehow, I didn't think Darcy would be our last. Somehow, we would have more. My heart quickens even now as I think of it, but back then I didn't have much time to contemplate anything too much. We might have finished having biological children, but there was still a lot of life to be lived and challenges to be faced. Now we had these children, these gifts from God, how did he want us to raise them up? We didn't just want to go with the flow. We wanted to know just what God had in mind for our boys. In fact, even from before Samuel was born, we wondered how we would go being parents and raising our children in the knowledge and love of the Lord. Relying on his grace was really the only way. We knew we were so full of faults, but God would help and direct us. So we sought him and his direction for our family. Little did we know that he would lead us on a path that only a few tread. As we listened for his guidance, his direction became clear. As one journey ended, another was about to begin.

Chapter 8

Am I on my Own?

Going with the flow... now what does that look like? Well, it's doing whatever everyone else does without giving it much thought. I can't say I ever was one to just go with the flow! It just didn't seem to fit my life. I guess it didn't fit what I thought the Lord wanted for my life. Not that it was particularly easy, sometimes quite lonely actually, but knowing I was on the right path for me brought a deep contentedness, even through the difficulties. The thought even inspired a song:

> There's a long and dusty road
> Full of potholes
> Full of stones
> But I know, the place it goes
> There's a highway on the side
> With grooves made by the tide
> Of the traffic
> That speeds by

My road is straight and narrow
Trod by no-one but me
It's not always easy to follow
But it takes me on
To the best
    I'm focussed on my goal
    Though there's always highs and lows
    There is one thing
    That I know
    I'm on the right road
    I'm looking to the end
    Not to the side
    Or round a bend
My road is straight and narrow
Trod by no-one but me
It's not always easy to follow
But it takes me on
To the best

The narrow road I thought the Lord might be leading us to in the life of our family was to home-school our boys. The thought of sending them off to be educated by strangers who couldn't possibly love them and know their passions and interests as I did, sat very uneasily with me. But on the flip side, I was at the time a pretty disorganised person. There was no way I wanted to mess with their education. What if I blew it? Their whole future would be at stake. No, it couldn't be the Lord's leading. There was just too much to lose if I got it wrong. There was nothing to do but to put the thought out of my mind.

If only it would be that easy! When the Lord has a plan, he doesn't give up trying to get through to us. We can shut Him out and justify why we shouldn't do what he's asked, but he won't stop gently convicting and encouraging. For me the conviction came as I read an article in a magazine about different methods of education. The article wasn't promoting one method over another, but was just laying out the pros and cons of the various options, be it public school, private school, distance education or home education. As I read the column about home-schooling, I felt a strong conviction that I shouldn't just wipe off the possibility of ever engaging in it, but that I should look into it more sincerely. The feeling was so strong that I knew to ignore it would be to my detriment. And thus the exploration began!

At this stage, Samuel was only about four years old, so Justin and Darcy were not yet born. Nevertheless, I found books to read on the subject and people to talk to who were already home-schooling. Most of all I prayed. If we were going to embark on this venture, it would only be with God's clear guidance. After a year or so I had become convinced that educating our children at home was the right thing for us to do. Far be it for me to lock myself in, however. I still wanted an escape clause or two! The first would be that I would give it a go for pre-school and if it was all too hard, I could still send Samuel to school for Year One and the damage would be minimal! The second was a bit cheeky, I think. I said to the Lord that if he wanted me to home-school, then I needed to know people who were just one step ahead and who I could follow and learn from. I couldn't know that God had just such a family in mind!

Somehow, while meeting with a few families at a park so the kids could play, I was introduced to a lovely lady who had two boys as I did. They were born in the same years, but earlier on, so were a school year ahead. What do you know, they had decided to home-school too! They hadn't been in town long, but it turned out that as well as home-schooling they even began attending the church we were involved in. I couldn't argue with God about this one. I had to give it a go. Unfortunately for us, however, the year Samuel had to be registered for Year 1 would turn out to be a year of great stress in our family, and not because of the home-schooling.

The year was 2005, we had moved into our new house a bit more than two years earlier, not long before Justin was born. Justin had just turned two, and a couple of weeks later school was supposed to begin. To make it really interesting, Nic started a new job at the same time, then two weeks into the job Darcy was born! Quite a messy start don't you think? And that was only the half of it! It seemed that Nic's new job was going to be very time-consuming for him for most of the year. By time-consuming, I mean he was leaving for work at 5:30 each morning, and not returning until about 8:00 or 8:30 in the evening six days a week. It didn't take long for this to take its toll on us all, though thankfully, despite Nic's absence, the schooling was going well.

Fortunately, Year One was a relatively easy year to home-school. We covered all our bases easily and had plenty of time for catch-ups with other home-schooling families at a park at least once a week. But not having Nic around was wreaking havoc in the lives of the boys, in particular Justin. Remember he was a good sleeper? Well his sleeping habits were about to be completely dishevelled. Let me explain why. With Nic leaving for work so early and arriving home so late, the boys didn't see him at all during the week. They were asleep when he left every morning, and were back in bed and asleep again when he returned. Although they would all say goodnight to him on the phone, it just wasn't the same as climbing onto his lap for a big hug and kiss and just hanging out with him before going to bed. Darcy was fine; after all, he was only a few months old and didn't really know what was going on. Samuel and Mitchell were old enough to understand to some degree that this was only for a while and that it wouldn't be forever, but Justin… poor little Justin.

While the others would get off to sleep quite easily, Justin just couldn't settle. We went from sleeping in his own room to moving in with his two older brothers. When this didn't help, we didn't know what to do. Every night he was getting up three, four, five or six times to make sure we were there and Nic was home. On one occasion I had already sent Justin back to bed several times and the last time I was extremely annoyed as I told him in no uncertain terms that he wasn't to leave his bed until the morning. Nic was still not home from work and it was quite late already. Eventually he arrived home and I warmed up his dinner for him as we caught each other up on how our day had been. Finally it was time for us to retire. As we opened the door to the passage which led to the bedrooms, who should we find on the floor, but Justin curled up and asleep! He knew he would get in trouble if he came out, but he had to know that Daddy was home.

He had broken me. My dear little boy. He preferred the cold hard floor to a warm cosy bed; he must have really needed his Daddy. From this point on I decided that to calm his heart and mind he would have to sleep in our room. We had set a boundary for our boys right from the start that they didn't sleep in our room. They could come in if they needed us and snuggle for a bit, but they always had to return to their own bed. Not anymore. Justin needed to know that everything was okay with Mum and Dad, and the only way he could know that was to wake up during the night and see us there. His mattress was permanently positioned on our floor, and his sleeping patterns returned to some sort of normality. When Nic's crazy work hours settled down, Justin went back to his own bed and we didn't ever have any trouble with his sleeping again. There's a powerful lesson right there about how much little children need to know that their Mum and Dad are okay and are always there for them.

BROKEN DREAMS IN WOUNDED HANDS

Over the year, we had to deal with a lot more than Justin's bad sleeping habits. Only spending time with my husband for one day a week was costing us a hefty toll. I felt that I was on my own. We had four children who all needed guidance and discipline when they were naughty, compassion when they were hurt, and love and hugs all the time. This I had to do all on my own. I can tell you, it was completely exhausting. One thing I was very grateful for was that I didn't have to add school runs to the mix. I was teetering on the edge, and that would surely have tipped me over!

Nic and I talked a lot about the situation. He liked it about as much as I did, which was not at all! But what could he do? They were in the construction phase of a new wind farm and the company were already far behind where they were supposed to be. Every day over the specified date of completion and the company would be fined a massive sum of money; that was why the employees were under the pump. Nic had always wanted to work in renewable energy, but was this really all worth it? We seemed to be drifting apart. Neither of us wanted it that way, but that was what was happening. One day a week together was just not enough.

Many times over the course of the year I desperately called on God and pleaded for some solution to my troubles. I knew he was with me, but I needed some help, some physical help. I contemplated taking the boys and moving to Perth to live with Mum and Dad until the construction phase of Nic's job was over and we could get back to some kind of normality, but every time I prayed, I felt a strong conviction that I had to stay. I obeyed, but life was so hard, often overwhelming. At least while I was at home, Nic and I could still look each other in the eye and see how much we loved each other and how much we needed to support each other. If we had put some considerable physical distance between each other, I believe the emotional distance would have expanded three-fold. I'm sure our marriage would not have survived such a distance, so I obeyed the voice of the Lord and I stayed. Praise God that he was able to hold us together despite the situation we were in.

As everyday life became hard, I'm afraid I had a tendency to reminisce over the past, and not in the most helpful way. I would rummage through my old photo albums from my Doulos days and dream of being able to do it all again. I wanted to be on the frontlines of Christian ministry, serving on the mission field in Africa. Oh, I loved my husband and my children, and was so blessed by a wonderful church in which I could serve the Lord through music and children's ministry. But what about all those unreached people in many of the developing nations of the world? How was what I was doing here having any impact at all on them? I thought on it so much that discontent began to grow in my heart. One day, however, I think the Lord had had quite enough of my miserable musings!

I was sitting on the bedroom floor and longingly looking over my photos when that familiar voice spoke to my mind, "You need to stop doing that. I have a plan for you right here and now. You need to stop looking back and get on with what I have placed in front of you!" The rebuke couldn't have been clearer. It was heart-wrenching to think that I may never again experience serving in the foreign mission field. But his voice was clear. He had given me a very important job to do. In fact, ever since I was little, I had often thought I would like to get married young and have children early. He had fulfilled one of my heart's desires and yet I was still longing for something else, something more. My heart sank as I realised that my constant reminiscing over the past meant that I was missing out on the good that God had for me at that moment.

As I pondered the words of scripture, through the grace and mercy of my Lord and Saviour, and with the empowering of his Spirit I found that truly for the first time in my life I could wholeheartedly say, "Lord, not my will, but Yours be done." It wasn't something which happened supernaturally. I had to make a choice to look forward and stop looking back. I had to choose to do it. Paul wrote in his letter to the Philippians, "Brothers I do not consider myself yet to have taken hold of it. But one thing I do: Forgetting what is behind and straining toward what is ahead, I press on toward the goal to win the prize for which God has called me heavenward in Christ Jesus" (Philippians 3:13-14, NIV).

God would help me as I moved ever onward, but I had to make the choice to press on. Was I living for what I wanted, and hoping for what I thought would be best? Or was I dying to myself to live for Christ? It was slowly dawning on me that it didn't matter where I was, what mattered was that I was serving the Lord with all my heart, always looking forward, not looking back and longing for what had been.

As I opened my eyes to what the Lord had placed in front of me, I saw my husband, my children. They were my mission field - to encourage Nic in his walk with the Lord, to teach my sons of the love of God and of all he had done for them in Jesus Christ, to serve them and others as Jesus served, washing feet, listening, caring, loving. If I was never able to lead a soul to the foot of the cross except my own children, I should be content. "Oh Lord, I've done it again. It was all about me. Fooling myself into thinking that overseas mission service had to be more significant than the task at hand. I'm sorry. Help me to serve as Jesus did. Be with me as I place all my hopes and dreams at your feet and leave them there. May your will be done and your kingdom come in me as it is in heaven. Amen."

On a very normal day, when nothing spectacular was going on, just the everyday things of life with four young children, God had broken through. I had once given my life to Christ, but somehow, I'd taken it back again. Now I gave it over once more. I didn't want it back. My way only led to discontent which was fertile ground for depression. I had been too close to that place and never wanted to go back again. "And we know that in all things God works for the good of those who love him, who have been called according to his purpose." (Romans 8:28, NIV). He had a plan and I had forgotten it. He was working out his purposes in and through me and it would all be good. That's what his word told me, that's what his Spirit in me confirmed. Everything was the same, yet everything was different.

So what did God have in store? If you say, "Take my life and do with it as you will", you can be sure that he will, and you'd better strap yourself in for the ride! Living life in Christ is not a stroll in the park, or a drive in the country; it's a rollercoaster of ups and downs, twists and turns and sometimes sitting still waiting for the next big dip! But it is the safest rollercoaster you've ever ridden, and I highly recommend it! In Christ, washing dishes and scrubbing nappies and wiping dirty faces and reading Bible stories and making meals is thrilling. It's serving Him. The scripture says, "whatever you did for one of the least of these brothers and sisters of mine, you did for me" (Matt 25:40, NIV). I'd not really stopped to think that in doing these seemingly menial tasks I was bringing joy to the Father's heart. I was serving his son by serving my family. Not that ministry stopped there, but that's where it had to begin.

Now the Lord had me just where he wanted me. I was ready to hear from him again. No voices this time though. No compelling conviction or research projects to explore. This time it was more like an ache inside. A longing which I believe was placed there by the Spirit. Our resolve would be tested and tested again. The Lord's leading would be as clear as before, yet so different from before. And that ache, that longing would not go away. It started with a picture. Just a picture on the cover of a magazine. Then the ache. Then the longing. Then the long wait.

Chapter 9

The Need, The Desire

The dark troubled eyes of the young child on the front cover of the magazine seemed to reach out and grab my heart. In some ways I felt like I was eight years old again and back in the lounge room at Wanneranooka staring at the TV and right into those hopeless, helpless and hollow eyes of the starving children. I felt compelled right then and there to find out her story. As I opened the magazine to search the pages for the article about the little girl, my mind started spinning. What was this that I was feeling? It wasn't hard to find the article, it was on the first page, being the editorial, and its title was, 'Caring for the Orphans of the World!' Not much was said about the little girl on the front cover. It turned out that she was one of a set of 15-month-old triplets who were adopted from Liberia into an American home. The whole article was actually about the plight of thousands upon thousands of children who found themselves orphaned and homeless in Liberia as a result of a long and bloody 14-year civil war.

Now Liberia had previously been known as the 'Gem of Africa' but more than the land was devastated by the extended war. Impacted beyond comprehension were the lives of so many desperate children. Some who were living in a particular orphanage wrote letters asking for a family to adopt them. "I sit and cry and sometimes I cannot eat because I can be thinking about my parents who was killed. I have to pray to find a new family..." wrote one 12-year-old boy. Another child expressed their heart's cry with these words, "I do not have no mother and father... sometimes I sit down and start to think about my parents but I cannot get over it how they was killed. I need a person who will sponsor or adopt me." Now how does that make you feel? Surely even the hardest of temperaments would soften even if only a little after reading such words. As for me, I melted like butter on a hot Aussie summer's day. I had a comfortable home, a husband who loved me and four beautiful boys. Surely I shouldn't keep these things to myself, surely if there was a need and I could do something to meet it, I should do all I could to do just that.

As my heart stirred, my mind spun; I'd always thought I'd like to adopt one day. Maybe this was why I hadn't felt that our family was complete yet. Maybe this was what the Lord would have us do next. The timing seemed right. Darcy was now about 7 months of age. If we could adopt soon then our adopted child wouldn't feel like an afterthought. They would know that they were just a continuation of our family. There'd been two years or so between each of our boys, about another two between an adopted child and Darcy would be perfect, wouldn't it? Then, we could adopt again two years later and my fanciful childhood ideal of six children would be a reality! Woah there little missy! Hold your horses! Wait up! I realised I was missing something: Nic's thoughts! So, I reigned in my enthusiasm until I had a chance to have a heart-to-heart with Nic. If adoption was to be, it had to be something we both wanted. If Nic wasn't partial to the idea, I would nip it in the bud right there. My heart kept stirring and my mind kept spinning; what would Nic's response be?

THE NEED, THE DESIRE

I really had no idea how Nic would react when I broached the subject with him. We'd talked in passing in the early years of our family life that one day when we'd finished having our own biological children, we might look into adoption. But would he agree that now was that time? Well, I could only bring the subject up with Nic; the rest was in the Lord's hands.

To be totally honest I don't remember the circumstances in which I spoke to Nic. He knew my heart on the matter as I'd talked about it on and off through the years, but I didn't really know the depth of his. I was about to find out. He wasn't surprised, he wasn't shocked, he wasn't disagreeable! In fact, he was more than happy for me to start looking into it. Oh my! We were of one mind. Although I can so easily be drawn emotionally into things, Nic provides a balance for me and is much more practical. That he was in agreement with me felt like a confirmation that I was on the right track. Then and there I committed our future to the Lord. My heart and mind spoke as one as I prayed, "Lord, our adoption hopes are in your hands. Please guide our steps and whenever the journey for us needs to end, please close the doors so we will know. We will keep moving forward until the doors are shut tight. May your will be done and your kingdom come in us and our family. Amen." From that time on, this has been my prayer, but where to now?

It seemed to me the magazine article was a good place to start, I'd go online and find out about adopting from Liberia. Looking back, I realise just how naive I was about adoption in Australia. I expected I would need to do a bit of research, but I was completely unaware that I was about to enter into a steep learning curve. I think it was so steep, in fact, that it actually took us upside down on some occasions, but more about that later. For now, let's get back to my ignorance! It didn't take me long to discover that as an Australian citizen it didn't seem it was possible to be able to adopt from Liberia. I wasn't deterred and looked further afield. My internet search this time led me to a site which listed orphanages all over Africa.

As I'd spent some time in South Africa, my attention was drawn to the orphanages there. Ninety percent of the orphanages were run by Christian groups, and one seemed to stand out to me over the others. It was called 'Shepherds Keep' and was in South Africa. At Shepherds Keep, abandoned infants up to the age of two were cared for. Although the staff hoped to find forever families for the little ones it wasn't possible for a large majority. You see the majority were sick, mostly with HIV AIDS, and would not survive. At Shepherds Keep they found a home where they would be clothed and fed, but even more importantly, loved and cared for, held and nursed until their little lives were no more. The staff treated these precious little lives with all the tenderness of a mother. I was awed by their compassion. Here was a job, unpaid for the most part, which would not receive much thanks in this world. These little ones couldn't express their gratitude to the ones sacrificing so much for them. But God was present with them. He was watching all they did. He was smiling on them.

I found their contact details and after working on an email to get the wording just right, which always seems to take an age for me, I sent it off. I wasn't expecting much in terms of a reply. I was just some random person from a place across the sea of which I'm sure they had never heard! Anyway, you know how the saying goes, 'nothing ventured, nothing gained', so I ventured and to my surprise, I gained! Yes, only a couple of weeks later I had a reply from Shepherds Keep. They thanked me for my interest and apologetically informed me that although they certainly did facilitate adoptions locally, they weren't sure about inter-country adoptions. Hmmm, that was a bit of bad news, but I read on. They did, however, have a Christian lawyer who was at that very moment working with the government to come up with a strategy for a way forward to inter-country adoption. They even gave me her details so I could contact her directly. That wasn't bad news, that was great news! It seemed I had to write another email.

If I took an age to get the wording right sending an email to Shepherd's Keep, imagine what it took to write to a lawyer! Nervously, after doing the best I could, I hit send. Too bad if it wasn't quite right by now, it was off in the net somewhere! It's a strange thing to be communicating with someone on the other side of the vast Indian Ocean whom I had never met. I had no idea what the outcome would be. But as I'd prayed that God would close doors if he didn't want us to go through them, I was confident whatever the outcome that God was in charge. Eventually I received an email from the lawyer explaining the work she was engaged in and the future prospects regarding inter-country adoption in South Africa. She was passionate about getting the ball rolling at her end, but her hands were tied in respect to the law at the time. In the meantime, she suggested that we contact our local government and see what could be done from our end. Meanwhile she would continue doing whatever she could. Not specifically on our behalf, but on behalf of all future inter-country adoptions from South Africa. What a lawyer, hey? Praise God for her heart of compassion and her tenacity to continue, even at personal cost to herself.

But if I was to start here at this end, where was I to begin? How about an internet search of adoption agencies in Australia? Would you like to know how many I found? Zero! There is no such thing as adoption agencies in Australia. If a couple would like to adopt, then they must get in touch with the relevant government department in their state. In our case that department was then called DCP: the Department for Child Protection. Ahh, now we were getting somewhere. Where would that be you ask? A very good question, and it wasn't really where we thought it would get us either! Paperwork is the actual answer. It got us to paperwork, but it was a start.

As in all good Aussie government departments, everything begins with paperwork. After speaking to someone on the phone we were informed that we had to fill in some 'Expression of Interest' papers and return them to DCP at which time they would be in contact regarding what we were required to do then. Okay. So what was required? More paperwork, and also some seminars: seminars for information, seminars for training, seminars for minor assessments. Oh my goodness. We were starting to learn that maybe adopting in Australia was not going to be quite as straight forward as I had expected; even just beginning the process seemed fraught!

Chapter 10

Getting Going in More Ways Than One

Although my thoughts would so often turn to what I hoped would be our impending adoption, I knew I had to apply a lesson I had learnt from my dear friend Cecilia. Years before, I remembered observing her life, albeit from a distance as I was home and she was still serving on the foreign mission field. I knew that she had a strong desire to be married, but her focus remained on Christ and on serving him. One day the news reached me that she was engaged! She had gone to visit a friend in Germany who had turned up to greet her with a huge bunch of flowers and a proposal of marriage! He had also served on the Doulos and was focussed on Christ's call to serve the nations. She accepted his proposal and they were soon married; their life of service together as one began. While she was oblivious to the testimony her life was to me, I had learnt a great lesson from her: while waiting for God's timing, keep serving and doing what you can wherever you are.

For our family, the focus on adoption couldn't be all-consuming, we had to consider the life we had to live in the present and trust our future hopes to the Lord. We had four precious boys and we needed to get on with the job of raising them up and directing them on the path the Lord had for them. Two things in particular we pondered: what we were doing and where we were living. As far as where we were living was concerned, as I'd grown up on a farm I was very keen to give our boys the opportunity to live on the land as I had done. Having space to explore, bush walk, contemplate and just get away from it all was so valuable to me as a child and then a young woman on the farm. I hoped to somehow be able to provide that for our boys. With that in mind, Nic and I began looking for land out of town. There were several properties which caught our attention, but one more than the others. It was only 17km from the town centre and it had a good balance of cleared land and bush, hills and flats. The downside was that there was no infrastructure! No power, no drinkable water, no buildings and not even road access yet! I was very keen to move to a place which was established, I really didn't want to go through the hassle of building again. If this was the place the Lord had in mind for us, he would need to confirm it clearly.

There's a bit of a story here but I'll try to keep it short! We visited the property a few times and decided to put an offer in on it. I wasn't certain, but nothing else had come up so we thought we'd move ahead with it. On the day that Nic met with the agent to express our desire to buy the land, the owner decided that he didn't actually want to sell it now after all! Okay. That must be the Lord's way of saying, 'No, this isn't the place for you'. We were disappointed, but as I wasn't absolutely sure about it, I didn't take it too hard. On we went with the search for land. The funny thing was, every property which we looked at afterwards I would compare to the one we didn't get! One didn't have enough bush, one was a bit far from town, one was too swampy, one was too hilly; it went on for several months. Eventually we had a phone call from the agent of the original property we had been keen on. Why was he calling? Another property maybe? No! He

GETTING GOING IN MORE WAYS THAN ONE

was calling to let us know that the owner was ready to put the land back on the market and that since we were interested earlier, he thought we should be the first to know about it. Now I was ready! It didn't have a house, power or water, but the Lord had used the last few months to confirm in us that it was actually the place he had in store for us. We enthusiastically agreed to purchase the land, even though the owner had dramatically increased his asking price. This was the place; the rest of the story was God's business.

By now, Nic was working pretty regular hours out at the wind farm. It was great to have a relatively normal life again, whatever that means! As part of his training, the company Nic worked for sent him to India where some of the components of the wind turbines they worked on are made. Here he and some of the others could learn more about them and therefore maintain them more efficiently. He was away for three weeks and we were so grateful for his return. Three weeks without Daddy is a long time in the life of a young child. Unbeknown to me, Nic had had quite an incredible experience while away. A couple in fact! One mind-blowing, the other stomach-churning, literally! The stomach-churning experience was his falling ill. He was so sick he was hospitalised, not something you really want to be in India! He could keep nothing down or in and was prescribed some heavy-duty antibiotics to combat whatever bug had entered his system. Although our doctor back home thought the prescription was a bit of an overkill, he assured Nic that it would be okay to take. While he was recovering in his hotel he had the mind-blowing and highly irregular experience which we could only put down to a supernatural intervention.

He needed a week to recover from the illness, so he spent the time mostly flat on his back in the hotel room. his energy levels had dramatically dropped and resting was about all he could manage. As he lay there on his bed one day, a vision appeared before his eyes. It was of our land. There was more than one dwelling on it and the land was well-established. Nic was unsure why there was more than one house on the land and the Lord impressed on him as he wondered, 'Your land is to be a place where people can come to find rest and refuge in Me. It is to be a blessing to everyone who enters. You are to establish a place for people to come who need to get away. It will be a place where I can minister to them and build them up.' I'm putting it into words of my own of course, but this was the overwhelming impression Nic received as he lay there on his hotel bed on the sub-continent gazing at our property which was thousands of kilometres away, yet was right there before his eyes.

Now I must explain here that Nic has always been very down-to-earth. This experience had been anything but down-to-earth! It was more, 'out of this world'! This being the case, he thought about it in his heart often but didn't confide in me for several months! I was thrilled of course, that is, after getting over the shock of knowing he'd kept it to himself for a few months, (I'd be blurting it out to whoever would listen if it was me!). The vision Nic experienced confirmed what I had felt in my heart since our offer of purchase had been accepted. Our property was not to just be for the benefit of our boys, so they could grow up on the land, but for the blessing and benefit of all who would set foot on it. Again, we found ourselves praying, may your kingdom come Lord and your will be done in our lives.

So that was the 'where' sorted out. Well, not the logistics, but the basics; now to the 'what'. What were we going to do in order to raise our boys up to honour God and have a desire to serve him? I had always wanted to go as a family to somewhere in the developing world. Our little part of Australia was so insular and relatively wealthy. We think we have difficulties and struggles; we think our faith is effective and strong; but when we meet and interact with people in the developing world our perspective inevitably changes. If we shut our eyes to the lessons the Lord would teach us, maybe we won't change, but if we're open to him we'll never be the same. I guess it was a big expectation to have, that my children who were only 18 months, three and a half, six and eight, would see and be impacted in this way, but I'm a firm believer that the Lord can capture the heart of the youngest child and inspire him or her on to great things. All we had to organise was where we would go and what we would do.

As it happened, our church supported a family who were working for Mission Aviation Fellowship in Papua New Guinea. We knew them reasonably well so thought getting in touch with them would be a good place to start. Their response to the possibility of us coming to visit with them for a month or so was very positive. With all the skills Nic possessed they could have used him up there for years. I didn't have quite so much to offer, after all, our boys would be with us and I would likely be busy with them, but still I was happy to help in any way I could. In no time at all it seemed, the trip was planned. I organised our passports and the required paperwork and we booked the tickets. Now we just had to wait until it was time to leave. Some would say we were crazy taking such a young family to PNG for a month, but we knew the time was right and we excitedly and a little nervously looked forward to our short adventure.

Twiddling our thumbs and sitting around waiting was not on the cards, however. As we organised our service trip, there were a few hurdles we needed to jump in regard to adoption. It was a requirement of the West Aussie government that we attend several specific seminars and training events relating to adoption. Most of these were held in Perth, for some we were allowed to teleconference with some other couples from regional WA. The last of these seminars was one we had to attend in Perth and was only a couple of weeks before we were to fly out to PNG. Needless to say, along with home-schooling and getting our house ready to sell, we had plenty to occupy our time!

BROKEN DREAMS IN WOUNDED HANDS

I flippantly mention the seminars, but some of them were actually quite taxing. We got the distinct impression from almost all of them that inter-country or even local adoption would most likely be a negative and very difficult experience and that we should prepare ourselves for a rough ride if we decided to continue past assessment to adoption. As I write these words, many years after completing those seminars, I can't really speak to the negative experience that adoption may bring; but I can say that a great deal of the experience to this point has been terribly harrowing to say the least. Yet with the seminars behind us and our desire to adopt undeterred, regardless of the negative spin, we looked forward to our trip to PNG.

Soon enough the time arrived. It had been a long while since I had waved goodbye to my family at an airport. It was quite surreal doing so with both Nic and the boys. Emotion rose as my parents prayed for us at the airport. The last time I had an experience like this was when Nic and I had flown to South Africa some ten years or so earlier. Wow, how much had happened in the last 10 years? I had time to contemplate it all as we flew the first leg of our journey to PNG. After arriving at Brisbane airport, we waited there for a few hours before boarding another flight to Port Moresby. As is usually the case in the coastal regions of PNG, it was hot and steamy with a very distinct, developing world tropical city aroma when we arrived. But there wasn't much time to think about how uncomfortable the weather made us feel. We hurriedly had to make our way to the domestic terminal to catch another flight to the highland city of Mount Hagen. Thankfully we were seated on another plane just in time for our last and rather interesting flight.

The aeroplane circled the cloud-covered airport of Mount Hagen for what seemed like a very long time. We knew that pilots flying in PNG always made sure they had enough fuel to get back to a major airport if the weather turned foul and the plane couldn't be safely landed at its intended destination. After flying in circles for so long we were pretty certain that we would have to head back to Port Moresby for the night. If the plane wasn't turned back soon there wouldn't be enough fuel to get us back! Suddenly the plane started to dive nose-first. There were some soft cries of surprise from among the passengers, and I noticed many white knuckles as people gripped their armrests tightly. The pilot had noticed a tiny break in the clouds. We couldn't see it, but he did and decided it was now or never to get this plane under the cloud bank and on the tarmac. The tension in the plane was palpable. Everyone seemed to be holding their breath. As suddenly as we began to dive, we were on the underside of the clouds with the tarmac in front of us. Wheels screeching as we made contact with the asphalt, the pilot braked hard. We were down! Spontaneously the passengers erupted in applause for the skilled and heroic efforts of the pilot. I said a silent prayer of thanks to the Lord for our safe dash through the clouds, he was our real hero and protector that day.

Our good friend Phil was waiting for us at the airport. It was interesting hearing his perspective of our dramatic descent to the airport. He mused that he could hear the plane circling around and around but couldn't see it through the clouds. He hadn't seen the gap in the clouds either and was as shocked as we all were when the plane suddenly appeared under them. He thought for sure that we would be turning back! Grateful for his familiar face and presence we preceded to the compound in which he and his family lived. Our adventure in PNG was about to begin. I hoped the whole experience wasn't going to be quite so dramatic as our flight had just been!

As it turned out, our time in PNG was not as dramatic as all that, but very challenging and stretching both to our lives and our faith. To sum up all we did there, we spent a few weeks in the large regional centre of Mount Hagen in the Western Highlands Province, then a few weeks in the small village of Telefomin in the Central Highlands Province. Nic engaged in much technical work in Hagen utilising his skills as an electrician and in electronics. I spent most of the time with the ladies who were home-schooling their children. On a couple of occasions, I organised some physical education type activities for all the children in the compound while the mums had a bit of a break. Although I couldn't really do much more, I was thrilled to be able to help in this small way.

The boys enjoyed spending time with the other children on the compound, especially those of the Snell family, our friends who'd planned our trip. Along with the fun and games, they learnt a bit about the developing world's difficulties. One was that they couldn't just drink the water from the tap or they would become very sick. They couldn't even use the tap water when brushing their teeth. In fact, I think it was me who succumbed to a vomiting bug first, then Mitchell! It only lasted a few hours, but was a definite reminder that we were no longer in a developed country. We should take nothing for granted from now on. They also learnt that in a developing world, security was much more of an issue. In Hagen we stayed in a compound which was quite safe, but at no time could the children leave without a few adults with them. I wouldn't even have left there for a short walk on my own. Although they were still very young, this trip was certainly showing our boys just how good they had it at home, as much as their immature minds could fathom, they took it all in; but they hadn't been to Telefomin yet!

Ahhh, Telefomin; what a beautiful, isolated yet welcoming, third world place it was. Only one airline would fly in and that was MAF. To get there the pilot had to navigate around many mountains. Yes, *around* mountains as they are so high the small aircraft, which can land on short hand-mown grassy runways, cannot fly over them without falling from the sky. The air is just too thin to sustain flight. Then landing the aircraft must be orchestrated with detailed precision. Get it wrong and you'll crash into the mountain at the end of the air-strip, or fall off the edge of the mountain! They must get it right the first time. Most strips don't have room to go around and do it again! The strip at Tele was a good length. At least compared with some others we had to land on. Since our flight was uneventful with one stop-over on the way, we safely arrived to a warm welcoming party of MAF staff and local dignitaries. After meeting and greeting them all we were shown to a small western style cottage which would be our accommodation for a few days until the pre-organised 'house sitting' arrangement would fall into place. At this point, all the resident MAF staff and their families left for a conference leaving our family and one other Aussie couple in Tele. We would be the only foreign residents in this far-away, underdeveloped yet majestic place for a couple of weeks.

I'm sure I could write a whole chapter on our experiences in these ten days at Tele, but for now I think a summary would be appropriate. Nic and a MAF employee named Kila from Hagen, spent most of their time working with the community leaders, sorting out the logistics of automating their hydro-electric scheme. Even considering the terrain surrounding the hydro-generators shed the practical work was pretty straight forward. What was difficult was the politics! Nic learnt a whole lot about how things often work in the developing world. Nothing is ever as straight forward as you might think. In the end Nic and Kila were able to automate the hydro-electric scheme so the residents of Telefomin and neighbouring Ankem could have a reliable power source. Until this time they never really knew when the power would come on or go off. As I'm sure you can imagine, that was where the politics came in, but we won't go there!

While Nic was busy working, I was busy looking after the boys in a very different environment than home! The first few days we were in a little cottage in which we faced some difficulties; the worst of which was that the mattress which Justin used on the floor must have had some sort of mould growing in it. Several times every night he woke vomiting. As soon as we moved out the vomiting stopped. That was one developing world experience I won't forget in a hurry.

Two more difficulties I would like to share showed me as the complacent westerner that I was, and humbled me immensely. The first was a church service run by women from the village for an international women's day of prayer. Most of the women who attended had to walk for several hours to get there and also to leave their fields for the day just to attend. I know that doesn't sound like much, but their fields were their only source of physical and financial sustenance. How many women back home would take a day off from their busyness, or take a walk down the street, let alone several kilometres around a mountain to gather with other Christian women to pray? Not too many. Would I? To my shame, probably not. Then there was the scripture message spoken by one of the ladies who had walked from the neighbouring village. I will never forget it, its impact was so great.

She read from Mark 10:46-52, one of the accounts of the healing of blind Bartimaeus. In a nutshell, Bartimaeus wanted to be healed by Jesus and wouldn't let the crowds deter him even when they yelled at him, "Be quiet!" In fact, their cajoling only strengthened his resolve and he shouted out even more loudly to Jesus. As a result of his not letting up, Jesus heard, responded and healed him. The challenge laid before us by this precious lady that day was to not give up in our pursuit of Jesus. When we are hard-pressed, do we cry out to Jesus even more fervently, or do we shrink back expecting he won't respond anyway? How much do we miss of God's hand in our lives by giving in to the voices around us? We need to be like Bartimaeus and when we are hard-pressed continue to cry out, 'Son of David, have mercy on me,' until he responds.

The other humbling experience was felt by our whole family, although most keenly by Nic and I. On the last day of our stay in Telefomin and

GETTING GOING IN MORE WAYS THAN ONE

Ankem we were invited to a special feast in honour of the work Nic and Kila had done. All the local dignitaries were there along with the other Australian couple and our family. We were given seats in a grass hut while all the villagers were seated on the ground outside. Although there hadn't been much food in the village for the week prior, the arrival of a MAF plane meant supplies, and these fresh supplies were extravagantly shared with us. They even cooked chicken for us, a supreme luxury which was rarely consumed by the locals. Lined up on several tables was a veritable smorgasbord of local food with the addition of rice and some sort of tinned fish. Behind each table were positioned ladies who served us with beaming faces. I felt like I shouldn't really have been there. What did I do during our time there? Nothing! Nic and Kila had done all the work, I had just been there and joined in occasionally with whatever the locals were doing. I didn't deserve all this. Yet continuously we were thanked for coming and for sharing our talents and lives with them all. Out of their lack, they abundantly shared with us. How could we respond appropriately? We were at a loss, we were undone, all we could do was to shake hands and hug as many people as we could.

The last thing I have to say about our time in PNG is that I never want to forget. I never want to forget the generosity. I never want to forget the discomfort. I never want to forget the isolation. I never want to forget the beauty. I never want to forget the people. To help me remember, I carry around with me a very special 'bilum' or hand crocheted bag made for me by one of the local young ladies. I only met her near the end of our time in Tele, but she shared with me her hopes to one day come to Australia and complete a discipleship training school with Youth With a Mission in Perth WA. We had used all our spare resources getting ourselves to PNG so we couldn't help her, and as it was, she had no resources to fulfil that desire. I pray with all my heart that she somehow did. I also want to mention Kila,

Nic's workmate who became our dear friend. Although we all treasured Kila, Justin and he had a very special friendship. Justin's eyes lit up when Kila walked through the door, and Kila's did the same. To this day, whenever Kila emails, he still asks after his dear little 'champion' Justin.

It all seems so long ago now, and I guess it is, but the lessons learnt still seem so fresh.

Life had to go on, however, and all too soon we were back home in Geraldton. So where were we before we left for PNG? We were about to sell our house, that's where! After four years living in the shed and four years living in the new house it had come time to sell up. I remember that during the years living in our beautiful house I made a conscious decision not to become attached to it. If God ever called us to go, I didn't want it to be too hard to do. Now, this is what I'd decided in my mind, but would my heart follow suit? Would I really feel okay about leaving the house I had waited for, for so long? I was about to find out. I won't go into detail here, but suffice to say, God was so good and I felt no sadness at leaving our home. It was a beautiful house with all the conveniences of a modern dwelling, but it was just a house. If Jesus was to return, it wouldn't go with us anyway, so why get too attached? For one reason only I wept. A few days after we left, I remembered the peach tree and the burial ceremony Nic had so sensitively led on the day of my second miscarriage. How my heart ached as I pondered afresh our loss, but by the far-reaching mercy and grace of God, I knew we were in the right place; he was leading and we were pleased to follow.

Regarding following the Lord's leading, at times I felt a little like Sarai, the wife of Abram in the scriptures. We'd left our home, but didn't as of yet have anywhere to live as there still wasn't any infrastructure on our land! We were able to house-sit for six weeks and then through the generosity of some good friends we moved into their attached granny-flat. It was only

GETTING GOING IN MORE WAYS THAN ONE

supposed to be for a couple of months, but as so often is the case with building projects, it took a lot longer to get our property ready for us to move in than we thought. Six months later, although we were barely ready, the time had come for us to move out. I think fondly now about the time we spent with our good friends, but it wasn't always easy. They are a family of six, we are a family of six and we all lived under the same roof for six months! Our family shared two bedrooms and a small living/dining room with a makeshift kitchen at the end. I couldn't believe that I had gone back to cooking for our family in a camp oven which was only about 40cm long, 30cm high and 30cm deep with two hotplates on the top! I think, however, I needed to be living in such a small space for six months to be grateful for a larger space on our property, even though it was just a tin shed! That was more than Abraham and Sarai had when they arrived in the land the Lord promised!

Looking back over the years 2006 and 2007, I can't quite believe that we emerged with all our faculties intact, especially our sanity! We had bought land, applied to adopt, completed various training seminars, travelled to Papua New Guinea, sold our house, moved out, house-sat, house-shared and eventually moved into a shed on our land. Not to mention keeping an eye on an elderly lady living in the place we house-sat, leaving the church fellowship we'd been a part of for ten years, forming a 'home-church' with friends, building infrastructure to a liveable stage on our land (including setting up independent power and water supplies), home-schooling (me), working (Nic) and just generally trying to keep some sort of semblance of normality for our boys! I might be starting to sound like a broken record, but I have to say it again, by the grace of our Lord Jesus Christ, the love of God our father and the sweet presence of the Holy Spirit we were enabled each day to continue on. One day at a time, one moment even, trusting in his plan, looking forward with all our being, never looking back, we were excited for all God had in store for us.

Chapter 11

Seeking Approval

By now I'm sure you might be wondering what was happening with our adoption hopes. Well, due to all the busyness of moving house, house-sitting and house-sharing, things were put on hold for eight months or so. Since we had settled into our new home, albeit a shed, we were ready to move forward again. The next box to tick on the government's adoption application list was the assessment. Before I expound on the trials and tests of assessment, there's just one thing I need to share with you. Now we were living on the land so to speak, I was making the most of going for long peaceful walks down and back our 2km track. Looking out over the unique beauty of an Australian coastal valley, I would walk and talk to the Lord and listen for his still small voice. On one occasion when I was feeling particularly low, I escaped to the isolation of the track and desperately pleaded with the Lord for an answer, "What's going on? Why am I struggling with life? Nic is standing strong in You, yet everything seems like such an effort for me. Home-schooling, parenting and even sleeping is hard." I felt that gentle voice prompt me to look up. The Lord had spoken to me through cloud formations before, yet as I raised my eyes skyward, I didn't know what I was supposed to be looking for. It had rained on and off through the day and the sky was filled with clouds. I've always loved gazing heavenward at the wondrous beauty which are clouds, but this time one little cloud drew my attention. It had the form of a person with a stick, or a staff. As it moved however it changed into the shape of a lion's face and then changed again into a very clear aeroplane. Finally, the cloud morphed into the distinct shape of a baby. No sooner had the images became clear, that the cloud dissipated before my eyes. What did the images mean? I had no idea. God had prompted me. That's what I saw! Somehow, I felt it had something to do with our adoption. What, I didn't know; but it gave me something to ponder.

The cloud picture stayed clear as day in my mind for a very long time. I still don't know what it meant, who knows if one day I think I will?! Almost a year had passed since that day and another exhausting and somewhat confusing couple of days were upon us. Yes, it was time for our adoption assessment. What a daunting word: 'assessment'. Sounds like some sort of exam. I guess it really was. We were put to the test. Through the ringer more like. Yet through the harrowing experience, God was working all the while. Nothing was going to stop his plans for us, though it took us some time to see that. Sorry, I'm getting ahead of myself again! So how did our adoption assessment pan out? For a while, not at all as we had hoped.

Since we live in the country our assessment was structured quite differently from most. Usually what happened was an assessor, a psychologist, was allocated, and over the course of a few weeks several interviews would be conducted concluding with the assessor writing a report for the adoption applications committee to consider for approval. As we live four hours from Perth, it wasn't very practical for our assessor to conduct a series of interviews over a period of weeks, so it was decided that she would travel to Geraldton and spend a day and a half interviewing us. Then she would travel back to Perth and a week later return to complete the assessment with another day of interviews. Talk about intense. It was extreme!

During the course of the first set of interviews we were grilled on everything from our childhood experiences, to our relationships with extended family and friends, to our financial situation, to details of our married life, to our living circumstances, to our parenting methods, to the education of our children and more. Going into the assessment we weren't too sure how our assessor would view our parenting methods. Over the years we have done several parenting courses and read varied books for tips on parenting. We couldn't be certain what the assessor would make of the fact that we occasionally spanked our children. Surprisingly, she wasn't particularly concerned. She seemed impressed that we had such a clear-cut plan for the discipline of our children which included many options with spanking being only one. As she asked us if we would be willing to read some of the latest research on discipline of children, we readily agreed. Although what we were doing seemed to work for us, we were always ready to learn something new that may be beneficial. Phew! I thought this was where we were going to come unstuck. No, it wasn't the parenting and discipline issue, it was the education issue.

As she left to head back to Perth our hearts were heavy with the knowledge that our assessor believed home-schooling was detrimental to the satisfactory education of our children. I knew my boys were learning all they needed to know, just when they needed to know it, in an environment which was rich with opportunities for further growth and development in the area of their education; but to our assessor we were somehow holding our children back. They must be disadvantaged by home-schooling, and she could see no other viewpoint.

We weren't ready to give up yet, not before we'd even finished our assessment! I contacted our home-school moderator and asked if she would write a reference for us. I spent hours researching the benefits home-schooling can bring and organised the information in a document for our assessor's perusal. If she was not going to recommend us for adoption on the grounds of our home-schooling, I wanted her to have as much information as possible so her decision would be made considering a wide range of facts, not just her viewpoint. Was it all going to be enough? Of course not!

Above all the work I was doing, I had asked many people to pray. I could only do so much. If our assessor was going to change her mind completely, it had to be a work of God. None of my hours of research would make a scrap of difference if God wasn't going ahead of us. So I worked and prayed and a veritable army of friends and family prayed along with us. By the time our assessor arrived back a week later I was at the end of my emotional limits. I was exhausted and stressed. So much for trusting in the Lord! I just didn't know what the outcome was going to be. I guess I still wasn't totally assured that adoption was what God wanted for us. Maybe he would end our journey right here and now. We didn't have to wait long to find out. We were armed and ready for battle! The moderator's reference and supporting documents were printed and set out on the table ready to hand over.

Nervously and with as much cordiality as we could muster, we invited our assessor inside for the barrage of negativity we were sure we were about to receive. Before we could defend our position, however, she started her spiel, "Over the last week I have done a lot of research in regards to home-schooling and I have found that on average children actually do better in a home-school environment than in a school. But this is not a general situation, this is specific. I need to know that your children fit into this statistic and are also doing well in their home-school environment." Well, you could have knocked Nic and I over with a feather! She had done a complete 180 degree turn around and hadn't even looked at the research I had pulled together! But there was a bit of a sting in the tail. "So I can be assured that you are providing a suitable education for your children I need a complete report of all you are doing with the boys, all the resources you are using, the people you engage with and all the extra activities they participate in. I'll take it back to Perth with me tomorrow and consider it as I make my recommendation." What? By tomorrow? We were praising God for his work in our assessor's mind, but I had a big job to do. A report which would normally take me several days to compile had to be completed in one night! But she was open to home-schooling! Only God could do that. He'd done what I thought would be impossible, surely I could now do what I thought would be difficult!

Working into the early hours of the morning I was able to complete a thorough report outlining the methods of instruction I was using to home-school, the resources I was using and the people who I was engaging with to help me in the process of educating our children. I also made it clear that the boys were not in the least socially awkward, but that they had an active and thriving social life participating in sports, church activities, Boys Brigade and many other social activities. I was starting to realise that the Lord was still directing our path. We had prayed, but I hadn't really believed. "Oh Lord, am I such a slow learner? Forgive my lack of faith. Help me to trust in You."

When eventually we received our copy of the assessor's report, we were pleasantly surprised but at the same time confused! The long and the short of it was that she was recommending that we be approved to adopt. That was the pleasant surprise; the confusing bit was that she recommended that we be approved to adopt a child who was similar to us, that is, a white child! Scratching our heads, we didn't really know what that would mean for us. After all, our application was to adopt from Ethiopia. As far as we knew, there were not a lot of Caucasian-looking children in Ethiopia! Where did that leave us then? We just weren't sure. It was really up to the adoption applications committee. What would they make of such a recommendation as this? Time would tell and we would have to wait some weeks to find out.

It was an unsettling time of waiting. Our adoption hopes rested on the say so of a committee of people who had never met us and who had to make their decision based on the assessor's report and our references. We had been given some indication that often applicants with biological children were not approved first time, but we still hoped and prayed that we would be the exception. Given the slightly unusual recommendation of our assessor, we were only slightly hopeful that it would come together for us. When we finally received the letter expressing the decision of the applications committee six weeks later, it was with much apprehension that we opened it. Our hearts immediately sank. The letter read:

Dear Mr and Mrs de Vries,

Thank you for your application to adopt a child. This was considered by the Adoption Applications Committee (ACC) at its meeting on the 10th March 2009. At this stage, on the basis of the information before it, the Committee is considering not approving you as suitable to adopt. I realise that this will be disappointing for you.

The committee values the fact that your family is functioning very well but believes that an adopted child with significant needs may well impact in a way which may disrupt the family's current functioning. Your large family, with the addition of another child, would make heavy demands on your time.

Furthermore, the Committee is of the view that your income at this point is insufficient to meet the costs of adoption and raising another child who may have additional needs requiring intervention from professional services. There is also concern about your geographical and social isolation from the mainstream community and mainstream ideas. The Committee also notes the absence of close extended family relationships.

Before a final decision is made, you have the opportunity to write to the Adoption Applications Committee to address the concerns. You may also wish to meet with or link up by phone with members of the Committee, who will elaborate on the Committee's concerns prior to you making a written response. If you choose to do so you may wish to take notes and then submit written material to the Committee within two months of the meeting.

If you wish to make an appointment to meet with the representatives of the Committee please call .... "

The tears welled and overflowed. It was very clear, these people who had never met us, never visited our home, never spoken to our family or friends or in any other way knew us aside from the independent assessor's report had passed judgement. According to them we had neither the time nor the recourses to be able to adopt. Living only 20km from a regional centre of 35,000 people was deemed to be geographically isolated and therefore we were considered to be isolated from the community also. And what was 'isolation...from mainstream ideas' supposed to mean? Not to mention our extended family, with whom we have very close relationships; they were just too far away to be of any benefit to us on the occasion of our adopting!

Compounding our grief, yes grief not 'disappointment', over their harsh judgement on us, was the fact that a lovely couple who had no extended family in WA and lived 60km out of the same regional centre as us had not long since been approved to adopt from Ethiopia with no questions asked! The emotions flowing began as grief and started churning into anger. Where was the consistency? Was there any at all? There was nowhere to turn but to our Heavenly Father. "Is this the end of the road for us? Does adoption end here in such a barrage of negativity?"

As I look back in my journal writings, I'm surprised to find that I haven't mentioned receiving the letter from the committee. What I did find, however, was a record of encouragement and correction from the Lord. On one day I quoted Romans 8:26 which states, "So too the Holy Spirit comes to our aid and bears us up in our weakness, for we do not know what prayer to offer nor how we ought to offer it, but the Spirit Himself goes to meet our supplication and pleads in our behalf with groaning and unspeakable yearnings, too deep for utterance" (AMPC). At this time I certainly had no words. I was so encouraged to know that God knew my heart and that it didn't matter if I couldn't form the words to speak to Him. Just calling on his name was enough. A couple of days later a verse the boys and I had committed to memory was going over and over in my mind. As I opened my daily devotional booklet that same verse was quoted as the verse for the day. It read as follows, "My dear brothers and sisters, take note of this: Everyone should be quick to listen, slow to speak and slow to become angry, because human anger does not produce the righteousness that God desires" (James 1:19-20, NIV). I can see even now that the Lord needed me to give over any anger I felt about the decision the adoption applications committee had made. Together, Nic and I had to look closely at their reasons for not approving us, and with the Lord's help and guidance clearly counter every point they had made. If I remained angry I wouldn't be able to hear the Lord's direction as we formed our response to the devastating letter.

Our first point of call was to organise to meet with the designated representatives of the AAC which we did as soon as we could. As we wanted to meet face to face rather than via teleconference, we made contact with the committee and organised to meet at the offices of the Department for Child Protection in Perth on the 16th of April 2009, just three days after my 35th birthday. If we were going to give this our best shot, we needed to look into the eyes of some of the people who had agreed on the decision and gently yet firmly explain why they were wrong. In the meantime, we would also work on composing a document with evidence from our lives that the claims of the committee were at best misguided and at worst completely unfounded. Oh, how we needed the Lord; how *I* needed the Lord. I'm as far from a confrontational personality that you could find, yet I felt such a strong compulsion to fight for the sake of our future children. With no natural ability for such a task I could only rely on the grace and favour of the Lord to move forward and confront the AAC.

As the prearranged date for our meeting drew near, we packed up for a short visit to Perth. With the boys settled in at my sister's place, Nic and I hugged them goodbye for the morning as we headed into the city to find the AAC offices where the meeting was to take place. Soon enough we found the address and parked. Thankfully we were early and had time to pray and commit our meeting to the Lord. It was comforting to know that many others were also praying for us. We only wanted his will to be done and his name to be glorified through us. It was quite surreal to think that our boys would be enjoying spending time laughing and playing with their cousins while Nic and I were anxiously waiting in a cold, undecorated, lifeless room to meet with the AAC representatives sent to speak with us this day. Yet here we were. Although I understandably felt nervous, I also felt a deep calm. God was with us and I knew that he was also going ahead of us. Whatever the outcome of this meeting, God was sovereign and I knew that nothing could thwart his plans for us, whatever they might be.

The committee members were very cordial to us, one in particular was even quite friendly. Thinking back, I wonder if they were nervous too. I don't suppose they knew what to expect from us any more than we knew what to expect from them! Although the initial tension in the room died down a little, it didn't completely dissipate. One thing I will say, it certainly was good to be able to speak face to face with at least a couple of people who were the decision makers. I felt as if they were finally able to glimpse the real 'us' and not just other people's impressions of us. All in all, the meeting went quite well, though one of the committee members had some very strange things to say.

One of the strange things was a question asked about why we wanted to adopt from Ethiopia. That, in itself, is not a strange question, but that was not the whole question. For it to make sense you must understand that we had been asked during our assessment if we would be happy to adopt an indigenous Australian child. The question itself took us by surprise as we had been told that the department didn't place indigenous children with Caucasian families for cultural reasons. As Nic had previously spent much time working in isolated indigenous communities, he had a quite a good understanding of their culture and the importance of extended family relationships to them. We felt that we wouldn't be able to facilitate the continuation of those relationships and the culture without considerable disruption in the lives of our biological children. The assessor understood our position and appreciated that we had thought it through. She reported accordingly. On this occasion however the committee member didn't seem to appreciate our sentiment so asked the following question: "Why do you want to adopt a black child from Africa, yet you don't want to adopt a black child from Australia?!"

For a short while we were speechless; what kind of a question was that? Did this person really think that because the skin colour of the Ethiopian

SEEKING APPROVAL

and the Indigenous Australian were the same it meant their culture and history was the same?! It was so bizarre! When the question had sunk in, we patiently explained again what we had expressed to the assessor. We understood the ways of the Indigenous Australian and the Ethiopian were very different. I would say that the most they had in common was the colour of their skin, and this was not an issue for us at all! During this interaction the other committee members sat silent. I don't know what they thought of the question, but they weren't giving anything away that's for sure!

When the meeting was finally over, Nic and I walked back to the car to debrief with each other. It had gone well we thought, and we joined in prayer again to thank the Lord for upholding us and giving us the words we needed when we needed them. We called Mum and Dad and briefly let them know that it was over. We would spill all the details when we returned in an hour or so.

It was wonderful to be together with family that night. We felt incredibly blessed to have what we did, and we so wanted to be able to share that blessing with adopted children. Whether we would or not, however, was only in the Lord's loving hands. Our part now was to wait again to hear from the committee with their final decision. Hmm, I hate waiting! Maybe the Lord was trying to teach me something. his timing is always perfect. If we commit our ways to Him, we can be sure he will direct our steps. Abraham had to wait a long time until his promised child was born. I was pretty sure we wouldn't have to wait 60 or so years, but even so, the waiting was tough. It was in fact three and a half long months before the letter arrived in the mail. If we were nervous to read the first letter, we were more so now! This was to be the committee's final decision. Would our family have the chance to know the joy of welcoming new members in, or would we remain as we were? Either way, what we were about to read would impact all of us deeply and for all time.

Chapter 12

LOOKING FORWARD

Dear Mr and Mrs de Vries,

Thank you for your application to adopt a child. This was considered again by the Adoption Applications Committee at its meeting on the 4th of August 2009, having regard to the additional information you submitted.

I am pleased to advise that the Committee was satisfied that you have shown evidence that you meet the required competencies for adoptive parenthood and have therefore found you suitable for adoptive parenthood. In accordance with Section 13(2) of the Adoption Act 1994 you are approved for the adoption of a child from Western Australia (but not an indigenous child) or a child from Ethiopia, up to the age of 36 months, who has normal care needs. An **adopted child** with normal care needs is defined as one who requires a level of personal, emotional and physical care consistent with that which would be expected for his or her age group and experiences. Care is essentially normal on a day-to-day basis, but some irregular lapses can be expected. You are not approved for siblings as the Committee considers that the demands of caring for more than one additional child would place too heavy a load on your family.

If you are dissatisfied with the AAC's decision and you believe that there is new information available regarding your suitability to adopt, then you may ask the Committee to review its decision under Section 42 of the Act. If you request a review within 90 days of the decision being made, the merits of your case will be considered. After that time, you will need to make a new application to adopt. Further information about this is contained on the attached page.

If you believe the Committee did not follow proper process in reaching its decision, then you may write to the Director General and seek a review of that process under Section 113 of the Adoption Act 1994.

Yours Sincerely.......

Review again? You've got to be kidding, right? We'd been approved. Praise the Lord! Although we'd hoped with all our heart that we'd be approved for a sibling group, we had so much to thank God for. We were happy to just be approved. If God wanted us to adopt a sibling group, he would somehow bring it about, I was sure. For now though, our biggest hurdle to date had been cleared. As I so often do, my joyous response to this long awaited wonderful news was to sit at the piano and write a song. The words flowed easily from a heart which was so thankful to the Lord:

LOOKING FORWARD

For years I have been hoping
Praying with all my heart
That God would send you to us
A new life for you would start
At times I almost gave up hope
Was I really in God's will?
Then he'd flood my soul with peace and joy
My hope would be fulfilled
You're worth the wait, worth the wait
What a joy to bring you home
Not too soon and not too late
You're worth the wait, worth the wait
I praise our Father in heaven, he knew just the time the season
To bring us to you, to bring you to us, we're so glad you're here
You're worth the wait

Try as I might, I couldn't squeeze a single word more out to complete the song. After 4 long years we were approved to adopt, but were told it would still likely be a couple of years until we would be allocated. I think the song will remain unfinished until I can hold our long-awaited children in our arms. I'm certain the words will flow to complete it then.

While all this was unfolding, the rest of our life had never stopped moving on, home-schooling dominated my days and much was happening in our family life. Not the least of these happenings was Nic resigning from his job at the wind farm. The work environment had become difficult for him and besides, he needed time to build our new home for us and our soon to be new family members! We had some reserves of capital from the sale of our previous home so we could afford for Nic to be without paid work for a while. Not only did the house need to be built, but Nic felt it was also important to set our property up as a business. Firstly, he tried growing hay, but the venture was unsuccessful. Then he decided on trying to breed dorper sheep. This led to more projects on the land which were not house related: tree planting, fencing, purchasing stock, establishing water points for stock, building yards and planting grasses for feed among other things. Remember that I mentioned that I hated waiting? Well, I'm much better at it now, but at the time the wait for progress on our new home took a heavy toll on my mental health.

Along with the stress of the adoption process, I had to try and deal with the fact that we would be living in a shed for a lot longer than the anticipated 18 months. When 18 months rolled around and we barely had begun constructing the walls of our home, I fell into a deep hole. Somehow, I lost sight of the goodness of God and began to focus on myself. My relationship with Nic was going downhill fast. I was placing my hopes for progress on him and in so doing was not trusting in the Lord. I think it had something to do with my hope being disappointed too. In Proverbs 13:12, the scriptures say that hope deferred makes the heart sick. I'd set my hope on an earthly goal and when it wasn't achieved at the time I'd thought it should be, my heart became steadily and surely more and more sick. I'd lost sight of the source of all hope. Not deliberately, but nevertheless I had. I prayed day and night, but my priorities were all wrong. My prayers were all focussed on me; on my pain, on my troubles. Believe me when I say, you don't ever want to go there. It's not a nice place to be.

Nevertheless, there I was, in fact there we were. Life at the time was like a dark, moonless night in the middle of a long, cold winter. It seemed on this night the sun would never rise. What could I do but hold on to the hope that eventually the sun would awaken the dawn and its warmth would thaw my hastily freezing heart. Oh, I knew how to put on a good face in public. Very few knew of the deep turmoil in my inner being. My pride got in the way of sharing my troubles even with my most trusted friends. Giving in to the subtle promptings of the enemy of my soul, I kept my silence and suffered alone. But I was not really alone. God was present. He was ever present, however I felt. As I was waiting and losing hope, he was waiting for me to look to Him and learn from Him. God waited many years for the people to turn to Him while Noah was building the ark, he had waited and given the Israelites chance after chance to change their ways and come back into his loving embrace. He'd waited for several thousand years for just the right time to send his Son to deal with the all-encompassing problem of sin. his waiting always had a purpose, to allow people to change, to turn back in humble trust and reliance on Him and his purposes. I was no different from the Israelites of old. In fact, you could say I was worse; I had their example, yet I still fell into the trap of self-centredness.

To be totally honest, I was comfortable wallowing in self-pity. Deep down I guess I didn't want to change. If I was to be humbled by the Lord, he may give me joy in my circumstances, then what motivation would there be for getting the job done. We'd be living in the shed with no adopted children forever and I'd be completely content. Now wouldn't that be terrible?! Well, wallow as I did, it really wasn't working for me. It didn't help progress things in any way whatsoever. It did wreak havoc on my relationship with Nic, but that situation would never work well for me or our family at all. Gradually, however, the Lord began to break through. I don't think there was a particular turning point. As the sun rises gradually behind a gently clouded horizon and the light spreads ever-so-surely until the sky is streaked with pink then gives way to glorious light which bathes the whole earth, the Lord's words slowly but surely worked in me. Over the years I've lost count of the times people have said to me, "You're such a patient woman to live in a shed for so long", but my reply is always the same, "If I was so patient, God wouldn't have needed to allow this circumstance in my life to grow it in me!" I am still learning to wait, but I have learnt to be content.

BROKEN DREAMS IN WOUNDED HANDS

The word of the Lord holds so much hope, if only I would take it to heart and put it into practice more often. I love the passage in the book of James in which he writes, "Do not merely listen to the word... do what it says!" (James 1:22, NIV). He goes on to say that someone who knows what the Word says and doesn't do it, is like a person who looks into a mirror, goes away and completely forgets what he looks like! How ridiculous! Yet that's what I had done; that's what we Christians so often do. Praise the Lord that his patience knows no bounds and he is willing to wait for the penny to drop, for the light to come on, for the message to sink in. I lost it for a while as I was waiting, but he didn't lose me; he just waited for me to return to the only source of hope which could ever sustain me, himself.

Ever so gently God broke through, my eyes began to look upward more often and inward less. It's amazing how your perspective changes when you look at things from a different angle! Not that my circumstances changed in the least, but now I was looking to Jesus, my endless source of hope. There's a story I heard recently which describes the situation perfectly. It unfolds something like this: There was once a little boy who had been misbehaving at the dinner table. After several stern warnings to get his act together went unheeded, his father had had enough. "Right," he warned in a foreboding tone, "tonight you will sleep in the attic." The boy's face turned pale, he had always been afraid of what might lurk in the dusty, dark depths of the cracks and crevices of the attic. He pleaded, "No Dad, please, not the attic. I'll behave from now on, I promise." "The attic!" his father announced undeterred. It was with shaking hands and knocking knees that the boy climbed the pull down steep staircase later that evening. He dragged his sleeping bag and pillow behind him, moving slowly in the vain hope that his Dad would change his mind. He didn't. After an hour or so of tossing and turning the boys heart leapt as he heard the quiet squeak of the attic door opening. "Hooray!" he thought, "Dad's finally given in.

It's back to my cosy bed." To his great surprise, his Dad silently entered and plonked down his own pillow and rolled out his own sleeping bag. He hadn't come to relieve the boy of his punishment, but share in it with him. From that moment everything changed for the boy. Although his circumstances remained the same, now his Dad was by his side he knew he didn't need to be afraid any more. He closed his eyes and slept soundly. This was like me. I was starting to see that my heavenly Father was right by my side in the thick of the turmoil. My circumstances were not changing, but my heart was.

If house building was going slowly, the adoption process seemed to have all but ceased! I knew God was walking the rocky road with us, but it was still hard. Again, I knew that I had to get on with life and trust that he had it all in hand. Believe me, there was a lot of other things to occupy my time. Of course, home education was still the biggest pull on my time but there were many other things I had the joy to become involved in. Once a term the boys and I joined with the 'Salt Shakers' a small group who sang hymns at the local nursing home. Then there were my activities at church. By this time, we were regularly attending a local church just eight minutes down the road which met once a month in a beautiful century-old stone building. On the other weekends we drove into town and fellowshipped with the same church family who organised the monthly local services. I ended up joining the music team in town, mostly playing piano and singing, along with leading the singing at the local service, first with my guitar, then on the piano when one became available! I loved being part of a music team again. In my busy life it was fabulous to have an excuse to practise playing piano or guitar! As well as music I found myself helping out with youth group and sitting on the parish council. Enough, you think? Never!

Our boys had each been members of the Boys Brigade from the age of five. Now, although it was a small company, they really needed more leaders. First Nic was asked to join as an officer, and then I was somehow roped in as well. It seemed the Lord had plenty for me to do. Some people go looking for ways to serve the Lord, but while we were waiting to adopt, he had dropped opportunities in my lap. I must admit, I was reluctant to take it all on, after all, when the call came that we were allocated our precious child, I would drop everything anyway and focus on them, just as I had each time I'd given birth to our four fabulous sons. Yet there was a need, a church family who needed my musical ability, a group of singers who needed the same, a youth group who needed a female leader and a section in Boys Brigade who needed to know the love of God through Christ. As I prayed, I knew that I could fulfil these needs for the various groups. I'm not a natural leader, but where the Lord calls, he gives the ability, so I took it all on. Through all of this activity and what was becoming quite a manic lifestyle, adoption was never very far from my mind.

I guess the Lord still needed to work on my attitude. I so often felt that all I was doing was just filling in time until I could do what he'd really called me to, and that was to focus all my energy on raising my children, biological and adopted, to love and serve Him. I'm starting to learn though that nothing done in service of the Lord should be seen as filling in time waiting for something else, some better opportunity to serve, something more significant! Every chance we have to serve Him is invaluable in the kingdom of God. It may be for a short time, it may be for a lifetime, but it is good all the same. Paul, in scripture, learned this lesson when he was locked up under house arrest. He had plans which didn't include being stuck in that place, yet he made the most of the opportunity right where he was. I wanted to be like Paul in this, but my heart still yearned so deeply to adopt. It's hard to explain. Like a throbbing ache inside which never quits. Never quite goes away, but sometimes is dulled by the medication of the task which is before me here and now.

Chapter 13

DOUBT

Learning to trust must be the hardest of all things. "Trust in the Lord with all your heart and lean not on your own understanding; in all your ways submit to him, and he will make your paths straight." (Proverbs 3:5-6, NIV). Trust, don't always try and understand, give him first place in all things, then he will move your life forward in the direction he wants you to go. But I wanted to *do* something. Surely there was something I could *do*? We were certain that we should adopt, but nothing was happening. Another two years went by since we were approved and still nothing. As we hadn't been allocated in those two years, we had to go through a review process. At our own expense we were required to undertake our medicals again to prove we were still fit and able to adopt, along with getting an updated police clearance to prove that we hadn't had any charges brought against us in the last two years which may jeopardise allocation. Then there was the dreaded paperwork to fill in again. Not as comprehensive as for the assessment, but quite a lot all the same. Oh, and I can't neglect to mention the changes to the program costs for Ethiopia. It just seemed to be getting harder and harder the longer we had to wait.

BROKEN DREAMS IN WOUNDED HANDS

When we originally applied, the cost of adopting from Ethiopia was 6000 Aussie dollars. Out of the blue we were informed that the costs had gone up and it would now cost $12 000. Was this the end of the road for us? $12 000 is a whole lot of money. We were saving of course, but if we were allocated tomorrow, we couldn't afford that much. Both Nic and I went to prayer. We'd asked the Lord to close the door if our adoption journey needed to end. Was the cost increase causing the door to swivel shut? Did God really want us to spend that much money on adopting?

The answer came swiftly and clearly. During our personal times of prayer and scripture reading, the Lord directed both of us to the same passage of scripture. At the same time, but completely independently! "I bring no charges against you concerning your sacrifices or concerning your burnt offerings, which are ever before me. I have no need of a bull from your stall or of goats from your pens, for every animal of the forest is mine, and the cattle on a thousand hills. I know every bird in the mountains, and the insects in the fields are mine. If I were hungry I would not tell you, for the world is mine, and all that is in it. (Psalm 50:8-12, NIV). *The world is mine and all that is in it.* As we shared with one another, Nic and I both felt the clear prompting of the Holy Spirit. We were God's children and everything in the world was his. He would provide all we needed just when we needed it. The embers of doubt had been doused with a dose of trust! 'Forgive us Lord for doubting your clear promise that you will provide and you have a plan.'

For a long time, our hearts and minds were at rest that the Lord was at work and that soon we would be receiving a phone call and a letter informing us that our file could be sent to Ethiopia and that we would subsequently have a child chosen for us. As before, however, the days, weeks and months rolled by without so much as a whisper from our case manager at the department that there had been any movement of our file. Again, time started to take its toll. Mostly on me I must say. When one day we received an email from the Department for Child Protection asking if we would consider becoming respite foster carers while we were waiting to adopt, something began turning over in my mind. What about fostering? Could God want us to go down that road? It certainly could happen a lot more quickly if we decided to apply to foster instead of adopt. Was this God, or was it me just wanting to hurry things along and welcome a new member into our family?

I shared my thoughts with Nic and he seemed happy for me to look into it further. All it took was a quick internet search to find the page on fostering in Western Australia. We had been informed in the email that if we chose to get involved in fostering, we wouldn't have to go through the whole assessment process as we were already approved to adopt. It looked like it might be a good option. I saved the pages for Nic to read before making any phone calls or sending any emails to enquire further. I needn't have bothered. God's voice came loud and clear! Not through that still small voice, not through my daily scripture reading, but through a surprising and thrilling phone call from our case manager!

The words, "your file can now be sent" were ringing in my ears as I excitedly flew out the door to inform Nic of the phone call. I threw my arms around him overwhelmed with joy that our hopes were going to finally be fulfilled. There were a couple of things we had to organise first, updated photographs of our family and our home along with a few other things. We got onto it as soon as we could and sent it all off. But nothing could stop my heart from soaring! It was becoming real now. Our paperwork was going to Ethiopia. We knew that it could still take some months for the file to be processed over there and for a child to be matched to our profile, but it was so tantalisingly close I felt I was going to burst with excitement. Of course I contained myself, but the boys and I prayed joyful prayers of thanks in our devotional time together. They had never given up hope that it was going to happen. They just believed it would. My faith had proven to be fickle at times, yet theirs was so steady. They prayed day after day, "Lord I pray for the adoption, that it will happen soon and that it will all go well". Such a simply worded prayer, yet jam packed with the simple faith of a pure heart!

* * *

There seems to be a common truth in our human experience. The higher you fly, the more it hurts when your fall. Well, we were all on a pretty good high knowing our file was now in Ethiopia and that sometime in the next few months we would be sent a photo of the child chosen for us. Since approval, the boys and I had been trying to learn some Amharic, the national language of Ethiopia. We had invested much time and effort into researching food and cultural practices of Ethiopians and had even tried to cook something which might be considered an Ethiopian dish. We'd done a project together and made a flag to display in our school area to remind us of the place our new family member was to come from. It all seemed so much more real now knowing that even as we worked on these things, someone in an office in Ethiopia may be looking at our photos and reading our profile. Surreal may be a more apt word to describe it. We were moving forward and were excited, and a little nervous about what the future held. What person in our situation wouldn't be excited?

Then came the phone call which knocked the wind out of our sails. It had been a couple of months since our file had gone and the government had decided to make some changes. As they had become increasingly aware of corruption in Ethiopia, a decision had been made to suspend the adoption program until their concerns could be satisfactorily addressed.

Our joy turned to confusion. But what did this mean for us? Our file was over there already. Well, it would stay there at this point. The government was sending delegates to Ethiopia to seek out reputable organisations with which they could deal and who they were confident would be aboveboard in all their processes regarding adoption. But how long would this process take? They couldn't tell us. Oh no, more waiting! "God, what is going on?" Through my confusion I forced my lips to pray, "may your will be done" until my heart could catch up.

Have you ever travelled internationally and had to transit in another country on your way home? When you're waiting in an airport between where you had been and where you're going, there is a sense of being in limbo. You're not quite home, but you're almost there. You can't hurry the next flight, you just have to wait. Ughh! You just want to get home! Well, multiply that feeling a thousand-fold and you might be close to understanding how we were all feeling at this moment. Almost there, but not quite! On our way, but not being able to do anything to get there faster! As the program with Ethiopia was suspended, so it seemed was our hope. When it was announced several months later that the program would be continuing with a new organisation, we were cautiously hopeful. As I researched the 'Grace Centre' my hopes were raised even more. The founders had moved from Australia to Ethiopia to establish an amazing place where single mums could be trained so they could work to provide for their children and where children could be cared for if their Mum had a job. Wonderful!

Why would a young Aussie family do such an amazing thing? The love of Christ compelled them, that's why! They were Christians from the Gold Coast! Double wonderful! They hadn't gone to build an orphanage, but in their work they had come across many orphans who needed care. They weren't actually licensed as an orphanage when the Australian government approached them, but they were in the process of applying to become so.

Wouldn't it be amazing to go to Ethiopia and stay with people who were of one spirit with us when the time came to bring our little one home? I was so thrilled.

But the rollercoaster had not stopped rolling yet. Again, days, weeks and months passed without any word. Then the worst news we had hoped would never come, came. Another phone call. With sincere care and compassion, Mandy our case worker informed us that the Australian government had decided that continuing an adoption program with Ethiopia was just too risky. The possibility of corruption was too great and the license for the Grace Centre to become an orphanage just didn't seem to be coming through. The Australian Ethiopian adoption program had officially been shut down. This time as I ran outside to tell Nic there was no joy in my steps. If I had sunk into the ground and had it swallow me up, I wouldn't have noticed. I could barely choke the words out before the hot, heart-wrenching tears fell. Nic held me tight as I wept. Was God finally saying that this was the end of the road? How could it not be? Our file was to be sent back and the initial money we'd paid to the program reimbursed. What about all that had happened in the past? The confirmation that this was what the Lord wanted? It had been more than six years since we had started the adoption process. We had weathered the ups and downs, jumping through hoops for the government, fighting for our approval, waiting and hoping for our 'God given' dream to be realised.

Yet somehow, I didn't despair, the ground didn't open up and swallow me. It was as if I was being carried by an unseen force over the gaping ravine of hopelessness. Somehow, I still had hope. I didn't know how or when it would be fulfilled, but I did know that God had already done so much. his word says that nothing is impossible with him. I believed it. If he could give 100-year-old Abraham and his 90-year-old wife Sarah a biological son at their age, surely to orchestrate an adoption would be a piece of cake for him! I just needed to keep on trusting and dying to myself and my timeframe. If I kept pinning my hope on him and not on my circumstances, he would sustain me. He would sustain all of us as we waited for his perfect timing. Instead of being overwhelmed by sorrow, we would be bubbling over with joyful hope.

As it happens, we had good reason to hope. Although there was now no inter-country adoption program operating between Australia and any African nation, there were rumblings of a new program. A delegation from the Australian Government had visited this country and was engaged in discussions about a way forward towards an agreed adoption program. Can you guess which country it might be? Go on, have a try! I'm sure you guessed right; South Africa! Joy of joys, the country of my heart! But it may take years for a new program to be established and for children to be allocated. Were we going anywhere? Were we sitting around twiddling our thumbs with nothing to do while we waited? Of course not! We always had plenty to do. We were getting older, with more wrinkles and grey hair, and there would now be a bigger age gap between our biological children and any we adopted, but none of those things would get in the way of us raising more children. Everything would happen just as planned and although a program with South Africa had not yet been established, I knew that as he did with Abraham and Sarah, God was working all things together for his good purposes.

Chapter 14

Abraham's Lesson

So what's the deal with Abraham anyway? Why do I keep referring to him and his wife Sarah? There's good reason. Firstly, he was a great man of faith, remembered for his obedience to God's calling on his life to leave his home and travel to a place God would direct him to. Secondly, waiting for God's promise to be fulfilled in his life took its toll and Abraham was persuaded to take matters into his own hands and help God to fulfil the promise he'd made to him many years before. This did not go well for him and the whole world still feels the effects of his impatience today. Thirdly, even though Abraham missed the mark, God still kept his promise to him. There is a lot I could learn from this man, his life and God's dealings with him.

Regarding his faith, scripture says, "Abraham believed God, and it was credited to him as righteousness" (Romans 4:6, NIV). What did he do? He believed the Lord. His belief and trust were enough to compel him to take his wife and leave their extended families and homeland and go to a place that God directed them to. When he left, he didn't even know where their final destination was! Yet he believed, so he acted. Every time Nic and I read the scripture James 1:27 when it says, "Religion that our God and Father accepts as pure and faultless is this: to look after orphans and widows in their distress and to keep oneself from being polluted by the world" (NIV), we believe it! When we read the words of the prophet Micah when he states, "He has told you, O man, what is good; and what does the Lord require of you but to do justice, and to love kindness, and to walk humbly with your God?" (Micah 6:8, ESV), we believe it. What can we do with Psalm 68:5-6 which says, "A father to the fatherless, a defender of widows is God in his holy dwelling. God sets the lonely in families;......." (NIV)? We can only believe it. As Abraham's belief led to action, so must ours.

Abraham didn't know his final destination or how long it would take to get there, but he left anyway. Nic and I didn't know where our adoption journey would lead us, or how long it would take for us to get there, but we had to go anyway. If our belief didn't lead us to action, what would that say about our faith? Maybe we wouldn't have as much as we thought we did in that case. Hebrews 11:1 says, "Faith is being sure of what you hope for, certain of what you do not see." If you're sure of what you hope for, and certain of what you do not see, you can keep moving forward, even if you don't know the final destination!

In Abraham's life there came a moment when time began taking its toll and the voice of one who wasn't speaking for God was louder than God's own voice in his heart. Of all people, it was Abraham's wife Sarah who encouraged him to take things into his own hands! Worst of all, he listened to her advice and did what she said. Wives, we need to learn a lesson from Sarah. Whether we think it or not, our husbands listen to us. If we're going to make suggestions which have such huge consequences, we'd better make sure we're speaking biblical truth, and not our own truth before we open our mouths!

ABRAHAM'S LESSON

The blame can't be laid solely at Sarah's feet. Abraham could have said no and that he would wait for God to fulfil his promise in his time; but he didn't. God had promised that he would make a great nation out of Abraham, but with no children, that didn't look like it was going to happen. I guess he justified his actions by saying to himself that he was just giving God a helping hand. Helping God sounds like a good thing to do, doesn't it? It sure is if he's asked you to do something. But if he hasn't directed you to do a particular thing, you're actually being rebellious by doing it, however you try and justify it. So Abraham had a son, Ishmael, to his wife's maid-servant. Many people today believe that the belief system of Islam was founded by descendants of Ishmael. Now that's something to think about, isn't it?

Back to Abraham, even though he tried to 'help God out', God still fulfilled his promise to give Abraham a child and at the age of 90 his wife Sarah gave birth to their one and only son, Isaac. If only he had waited and not listened to any voice but the voice of the Lord. So many times during our adoption journey so far, I have had thoughts to 'help God out', usually considering fostering. At these times I'm so grateful that Abraham has gone before. I can see that it didn't work out well for him or Sarah and it only brought hurt and trouble to the family. Waiting is the best option. Even if it's for a lifetime, we're better off waiting. God will work his plan out just as he promises in his word. In the words of the old hymn we just need to "Trust and obey, for there's no other way to be happy in Jesus, but to trust and obey".

I know that 'trusting' and 'obeying' is much easier said than done, but it all begins with a choice; will I choose to put God first in my life, or myself? If I choose God, he pulls out all the stops to enable me to trust and obey. How do I know this? Well, he tells me so in his word. Here are some examples:

"His divine power has given us everything we need for a godly life through our knowledge of him who called us by his own glory and goodness" (2 Peter 1:3, NIV).

"Trust in the Lord with all your heart and lean not on your own understanding, in all your ways submit to Him and he will make your paths straight" (Proverbs 3:5-6, NIV).

"Keep your lives free from the love of money and be content with what you have, because God has said, "Never will I leave you; never will I forsake you. So we can say with confidence, "The Lord is my helper; I will not be afraid. What can mere mortals do to me?" (Hebrews 13:5-6, NIV).

So in our hearts we must choose to trust, not relying on fickle feelings, but on the steadfast word of God.

When doubt assaults our mind, we need to look to God's word and trust Him with our whole heart. His word reminds us that he is ever faithful to fulfil his promises to his people. Abraham messed up big time, yet God still kept his promise to make a great nation out of him. Through him, all of mankind has surely been blessed by the one who was born of his line, the long-awaited Messiah, Jesus. I am so encouraged by God's dealings with Abraham. Whenever I have doubted God's promises, or started down a road which the Lord didn't lead me on, I haven't prevented God from fulfilling his promises through me. Maybe I might have made things hard on myself sometimes, just as Abraham and Sarah did, but that doesn't mean that it's all over. King David understands this, as is seen in his writing in Psalm 145:13-19, "Your kingdom is an everlasting kingdom, and your dominion endures through all generations. The Lord is trustworthy in all he promises and faithful in all he does. The Lord upholds all who fall and lifts up all who are bowed down. The eyes of all look to you, and you give them their food at the proper time. You open your hand and satisfy the desires of every living thing. The Lord is righteous in all his ways and faith-

ABRAHAM'S LESSON

ful in all he does. The Lord is near to all who call on him, to all who call on him in truth. He fulfils the desires of those who fear him; he hears their cry and saves them." (NIV)

So where does this leave us? We learn from Abraham that we need to continue to be obedient to God's call on our lives regardless of the cost to us. We need to wait patiently for God to fulfil his promises to us and remember that at any time we can go to his word if time is taking its toll and we start to doubt his faithfulness. Unlike Abraham, we shouldn't try and 'help God out', but should always just trust, (not always easy, but scripture gives us much encouragement to help us out!). Finally, if we do miss the mark, which, let's face it, is quite likely on occasion, we don't ever have to be discouraged that God has given up on us. As he fulfilled his promise to Abraham, he will fulfil his promises to us. We can be sure of this as he makes it very clear in his word that this is the case. Knowing this truth there are only two things left for us to do. Regardless of the cost, we must trust and obey.

Chapter 15

South Africa – A New Direction; Or Is It?

So this is where we find ourselves, learning to trust and obey, taking every day as it comes and trying to lean fully on the love and grace which the Lord extends to us in Jesus Christ. If we are in God's will, he will work it all out in his way and in his time. A childhood favourite song of mine, which Psalty the Singing Song Book used to sing, called "In his Time" expresses so well the attitude we should always strive to have. The lyrics reflect the words of the writer of Ecclesiastes when he states "He (God) has made everything beautiful in its time. He has also set eternity in the human heart; yet no one can fathom what God has done from beginning to end." (NIV), and Psalm 25:4 "Show me your ways, Lord, teach me your paths." (NIV)

I used to love singing that song as a child, and as an adult I knew I needed to take the words to heart more than ever. Although adoption news had been coming in less and less, there had been some incremental changes, which we couldn't help but see as the hand of God, working towards the fulfilment of his purposes. Let me explain. I mentioned in a previous chapter that there were rumblings of a program being opened with South Africa. Well, when the program with Ethiopia was closed by the Australian government, our sights drifted to SA. We felt so strongly that Africa was the place for us, and since there wasn't any other active programs with Africa, a new program with SA would be our only hope of adopting. Mandy our case worker mentioned at one stage that she would support us 100% if we chose to focus on South Africa, but she made it clear, that as this was all so new, we were in for a bit of a rollercoaster ride. To date, we have certainly experienced lots of ups and downs, lots of unknowns, and lots of periods of complete and utter nothingness!

But I'm getting ahead of myself. At this point in time, we were only at the beginning of our South African adoption journey. The stark words 'roller coaster' kept surfacing in my mind. What exactly would that mean? Many highs and lows I guess. The first low was quite a shocking one. As always seems to be the case, we were informed of the potential problem in a phone call from Mandy. She was completely supportive of our switching our country of preference to South Africa and was therefore looking over our paperwork. In doing so, she discovered something that neither she nor we had been aware of. If seems that our original approval for inter-country adoption had been exclusively for Ethiopia! I didn't know if I'd heard her correctly. I was sure we had been approved for general inter-country adoption. If we had have been, we could just ask for our file to be sent to another country and it could be arranged. But being approved exclusively for Ethiopia meant that we would have to apply to the Adoption Application Committee for an 'open' approval. Without it, we could forget adopting from South Africa, in fact, we could forget our inter-country adoption journey continuing, period.

As it happens, our two-year update was about due. Yes, eight years after enquiring we again had to have updated police clearances and medicals

SOUTH AFRICA - A NEW DIRECTION; OR IS IT?

done, along with all the usual paperwork. Mandy suggested that as we were updating our paperwork anyway, we should request a different approval. In fact, since we wanted to change our inter-country approval, she suggested that if there was anything else we wanted to change, we should request those changes at the same time. And there certainly were some other changes we hoped for in our approval status, namely approval for a sibling group and for the age of the child to be increased to be closer in age to Darcy. Well, 'one in, all in' as the saying goes. As long as it didn't end up being 'one out, all out'! We certainly didn't want our two-yearly update to become the end of our adoption journey.

Now, normally significant changes like the ones we wanted would require us to be assessed all over again. A daunting thought and you can be sure we didn't want to go down that road again! But maybe there was another option. Our faithful advocate Mandy suggested that she could come up to Geraldton and do the reassessment herself. After all, she knew us better than anyone in the department. We thought that was a wonderful idea, but would the AAC agree? They hadn't always seen things the way we did. While she took the idea to the committee, we took it to our Lord in prayer. Since our experiences to date with the AAC were not always positive, we prayed the Lord would somehow intervene and they would approve our two-yearly update and reassessment to be done by Mandy. More waiting. You'd think we'd be used to it by now, wouldn't you? This time the wait was only about a week. Mandy called the moment she'd heard the news; they'd agreed to let her come here and reassess us herself! My heart was filled with gratitude for her, and I let her know how much it meant to us to be able to meet with her in our home. I was also overwhelmed with gratitude to our Lord. He was again confirming that he was still leading us on this ever-changing adventure and that we could surely trust in Him.

So a date was set for the re-assessment and all we had to do was tidy up. Ughhh! You could say that we liked the 'lived in' look, or in fact you could say that we are not altogether the most tidy people you've met. Living in a shed doesn't help. The longer I lived there, the more my care-factor reduced! What difference does it make anyway, it's only a shed! On the other hand, it is our home. In any case, we needed to make sure it looked good for our meeting. Inside there was sorting stuff, vacuuming, sweeping, mopping, cleaning, dusting and lots of other little jobs that often fall off the radar in a busy life. Then there was the outside to tidy up.

For some reason we decided now would be a good time to move the leftover straw bales, all 300 or so of them, out from the shed across the driveway to a cleared patch of bush a couple of hundred metres away. I think Nic must have been caught up at work because my recollection is that the boys and I worked hard for many hours loading bales, driving the short distance, offloading and neatly stacking them and doing it all over again, and again, and again countless times until they were all successfully removed. Oh, but that wasn't the end of the job. Oh no! Then we had to clean up and remove the pallets the straw had been stored on and finish the job off by raking, sweeping and gathering up the ute loads of half-mouse-eaten straw scraps left on the ground of the shed and removing them to a different location also. Phew, were we glad to see the back of that job. The timing hadn't been brilliant, but the satisfaction of knowing it was done and wouldn't need to be done again was fantastic!

In our usual disorganised fashion, we finished all we wanted to do only an hour or so before Mandy appeared at the top of the driveway! Wow, that was close; but we were ready. We were showered, dressed nicely and smelling sweet, the dogs were tied up, the pet sheep shut in a nearby paddock, the kettle was boiling for a cup of tea and some home-baked bikkies

SOUTH AFRICA - A NEW DIRECTION; OR IS IT?

were arranged on a plate on the dining table. Mandy had never been to our home before, and we wanted her first impression to be a good one.

We needn't have worried. She put us at ease right away with her lovely smile and her relaxed manner. The boys occupied themselves with Lego, books, computer games or outside play while Mandy, Nic and I began the mini assessment. There was a lot to cover, but it all went quite smoothly. By the end of the meeting we were all a bit drained, yet feeling satisfied that we had been able to share freely and articulate well our reasons for the changes we wanted to see in our approval. It certainly had been a lot less stressful than our original assessment which had left us despondent and pessimistic about our chances of approval. This time we felt hope rising and the stress drain away even as we waved good-bye to Mandy while she drove back up the track towards town.

Chapter 16

Life Doesn't Slow Down

So there we were, waving good-bye to Mandy. We couldn't be sure of the outcome of our meeting, but there was a certain peace that seemed to settle deep in our souls that God was in control and whatever was going to happen would be a part of his will. Nic and I had only to complete some paperwork and send it off by a certain date so the committee could peruse it along with Mandy's report and recommendation. There had been a bit of a hold up with some of the medical reports, but we received them with plenty of time to post it all down to Perth. I thought that the best thing to do was to send it via registered mail as there was a lot of personal information enclosed and it was so very important that they didn't get lost in the abyss of the postal system somewhere! There was, however, one problem with that. Registered mail takes longer to get to where it needs to go. I had sent the papers with a week to spare, surely that would be plenty of time for them to travel the 400km to Perth. Well, you'd think so, wouldn't you? I did! It seems that again I was putting my faith in man's systems (namely Australia Post) rather than trusting in God, how silly of me!

BROKEN DREAMS IN WOUNDED HANDS

Of course it was silly trusting in something run by mere humans, as there is then the factor of error or misunderstanding to consider. The day came when Mandy needed the paperwork, and it wasn't there. Where was it? Somewhere in that abyss I mentioned earlier! Mandy was able to get a day's grace from the AAC, but I still needed to find the paperwork for her. After many phone calls to various post offices in the vicinity of her offices, I eventually found it. Then, after several missed calls I was able to get hold of Mandy and point her in the direction of the post office which held the papers. With no time to spare she picked up the paperwork and was on her way. Why is it so often that these things happen at the last minute? Is it so we will trust more completely in the Lord? I just wish I could give it all over to him and stop leaning on my humanity; 'Lord, when will I ever learn?"

Unlike previous occasions, we didn't have to wait too long for our approval to come through. This time we received an 'open' approval for inter-country adoption of a single child up to the age of six, with mild special needs, or a sibling group of two with no special care needs. As we found out later, however, most children needing adoptive families were HIV positive. As a result, we were required to provide a letter from a local medical doctor stating their willingness to support us in the event that we adopted a child with this condition. What do you know? Our family doctor was actually originally from South Africa and had spent time working in a children's hospital there! If you know anything about HIV/AIDS in Africa, then you'd already know that in her work in the children's hospital, our doctor gained much experience working with HIV/AIDS patients. When we asked her if she'd be willing to support us, she expressed surprise that the Australian government would even let a child be adopted into Australia who had the condition (it would be an expensive exercise for the government in regards to the lifetime of medication a person would need); having said that, she went on to warmly agree to support us if it was necessary.

LIFE DOESN'T SLOW DOWN

By now it was about the middle of the year 2015, 10 years since we began the adoption process. It really felt that for the first time things were moving forward at a steady pace in regard to adoption. In other positive ways life was moving forward too. In mid-November that same year, my sister Kathryn and her family came up to help with the final push to finish the house and to help with some packing. It was a fruitful visit and in late November our family finally moved into our new home, eight years after moving into the shed on our small farm! You should have seen the dust accumulated under some of the furniture. Actually, scratch that, it's a good thing you didn't! There were a few friends from church, Peter and his sons, Matt and Tom, who helped us move. I've got to say, it was a bit embarrassing to have all the filth exposed, but they didn't seem to bat an eyelid and just pitched in. By the end of the day we were all sweaty and dirty with dust under our nails and up our noses! It was so satisfying though to see our furniture in its new home, and even more so to sleep in our new home. It'd been a long eight years in many ways.

Back to the adoption process, it wasn't long after our new approval that our file was sent to South Africa. We were told our file was one of only three which were chosen, and that we were on the top of the list! I've got to say though, when we received the news that our file had arrived in South Africa soon after, I was a bit numb. I'd been here before. I suppose I wasn't allowing myself to celebrate, expecting a long journey yet. I was right to feel this way. After a few months we had to do more paperwork to update our file so our approval didn't lapse! We gritted our teeth and got it done. Then there came a long, long silence.

Chapter 17

Simply Trusting

Simply trusting every day
Trusting through a stormy way
Even when my faith is small
Trusting Jesus, that is all
    Trusting as the moments fly
    Trusting as the days go by
    Trusting Him whate'er befall
    Trusting Jesus, that is all
Brightly doth his Spirit Shine
Into this poor heart of mine;
While he leads I cannot fall;
Trusting Jesus, that is all

Singing if my way is clear,
Praying if the path be drear;
If in danger for Him call;
Trusting Jesus, that is all

Trusting Him while life shall last,
Trusting Him till earth be past
Till within the jasper wall,
Trusting Jesus, that is all
    Trusting as the moments fly
    Trusting as the days go by
    Trusting Him whate'er befall
    Trusting Jesus, that is all

©Public Domain

What does it mean to trust in God and how can we do it? What does it mean to have hope and how can we live in it? I find myself so often asking those questions. Sometimes the answers are clearer than at other times, but as I live each day with God by my side and ponder on the scriptures, his Spirit unfolds more and more of his truth to me. I don't think anyone could give you a formula to follow so you could tick the box which says, 'Now I trust fully in God' or 'Now I will always hope and never doubt', but I know that we all can get better and better at both if we always keep our eyes on Jesus. There is a reason the scriptures call Him the "Author and Perfector" of our faith (Hebrews 12:2). Without Him there is no eternal hope and no-one in whom we can trust completely.

Although each of us has been created in the image of God, we all have a completely unique path to tread in our life's journey. But we also have the Holy Spirit, the Bible and each other, all of which can teach us and help guide us to a closer walk with the Lord and a deeper understanding of God's purposes for us. With this in mind, I'd like to encourage you with these words, 'Never give up'. Don't give up on God. I've been walking with Him since I was a young child and have loved Him for as long as I can remember, yet the understanding of his deep love for me is still in its infancy.

> *Jesus loves me this I know*
> *For the Bible tells me so*
> *Little ones to Him belong* (and big ones too!)
> *They are weak but he is strong.*
> *Yes Jesus loves me.*
> *Yes Jesus loves me.*
> *Yes Jesus loves me.*
> *The Bible tells me so.*
> ©Public Domain

These must be about the most profound words in the universe. But how does Jesus want me to respond to his love? How does a mother want her child to respond to her love? Does she want gifts? Does she want to be served by her child? Does she want money? Does she want.....? Some of these things are nice, but what she really wants is to know her child simply loves her back. Is that not what God wants of me? To love Him back? To trust in Jesus more and more is to love him more and more. What did he say was the greatest commandment? To "Love the Lord your God with all your heart and with all your soul and with all your mind", and close behind, "Love your neighbour as yourself. All the Law and the Prophets hang on these two commandments" (Matthew 22:38-40 NIV). If all the law is summed up in these two profound commands, then these are what the followers of Jesus should be about.

Have you ever seen a little child jump from a height into their parent's arms? They just expect that they will be caught as they throw themselves off whatever apparatus they happen to be playing on! They have complete trust in their parent's love and ability to catch them. On the other hand, a child who has never known the security of a loving mum and dad would never attempt such a brash action. If they're not sure of their parent's love, they can't be sure they will be caught if they were to jump. Does God not call us his children? Has he not proven his love for us through the giving of his precious Son? We can throw ourselves on his grace and mercy and know beyond the shadow of a doubt that he will catch us. But we need to be assured of his love for us, and we need to desperately want to be caught up in his arms. If we're not, any height will be too high to jump from, even if it's only one step off the ground.

Asaph articulated it so well as he wrote in the Psalms:

> "Whom have I in heaven but you?
> And earth has nothing I desire besides you.
> My flesh and my heart may fail, but God is the strength of
> my heart and my portion forever." (Psalm 73:25-26, NIV)

Asaph did not write these words from a position of comfort and ease. He knew trouble and difficulty when so many others seemed to experience the opposite. Yet when he looked at his calamity and the ease of others from an eternal perspective instead of an earthly one, he was able to declare:

> "But as for me, it is good to be near God.
> I have made the Sovereign Lord my refuge;
> I will tell of all your deeds." (Psalm 73:28, NIV)

Trusting the Lord is not easy, though it is necessary. It does come with a caveat, however, it's got to be on his terms. I shouldn't trust that God will do whatever I want him to do. I shouldn't trust that he will enable my will to be done. I want to adopt, so God will make it happen. Umm, not necessarily. James writes, "Come now, you who say, "Today or tomorrow we will go to such and such a city, and spend a year there and engage in business and make a profit." Yet you do not know what your life will be like tomorrow. For you are just a vapor that appears for a little while, and then vanishes away. Instead, you ought to say, "If the Lord wills, we will live and also do this or that." (4:13-15, NASB)

So our trust in Christ is in his completed work on the cross and his resurrection from the dead. Because of this we can trust that our salvation is secure (John 6:37), that our future is sealed (1 Peter 1:3-4), that our hope of eternal life with him is certain (Hebrews 10:19-22), that he will walk with us every day (Matt 28:20), that his grace is all we need (2 Corinthians 12:9), that the world will bring us trouble but that he has overcome this world (John 16:33), that if we obey him, we will have his peace (John 14:23-27). We don't read anywhere that our dreams will be fulfilled (even if they are good dreams), or that our human desires for things will be satisfied (even if they are good things we desire).

Does trusting him look a little different to you now?

Chapter 18

Fostering

Yes, trusting in Christ is not about my will, it's about his. Would I trust him in the silence as well as in the noise? Maybe you can make up your own mind about whether I did that well or not! To fill the silence mentioned at the end of Chapter 16, we decided to pray about whether we should apply to be foster carers. After praying, talking to people and doing a bit of research we came to the conclusion that it would be worth giving fostering a go while we were waiting to adopt. Darcy was now 13 and I felt out of practice with little children so it would be a good opportunity to get the hang of it again. You'll never guess what being approved to be foster carers entailed - more interviews, house inspections and training of course!

Funny story: after we'd applied to become foster carers, we had a phone call from a lady from the Department for Child Protection who was going to oversee us and our application. She had a sweet French sounding name and spoke with a lovely English accent. Her manner over the phone put me at ease right away. We talked a little and she asked if she could come out to our home to meet us and to inspect our house and property. We settled on a date and locked it into our diaries. On the day of her visit, I made sure the house was clean and tidy, some home-made nibbles were prepared, and the kettle was hot. I had explained how to get to our place and suggested that she turn her GPS off and just follow my directions. We know from the experience of others that a GPS takes you to the middle of a paddock near the far corner of our property where it tells you to get out of your car and walk 150m through the paddock before reaching your destination. You can't even see our house from that corner of our property! Sure enough, our friendly English lady from DCP tried to follow her GPS. As a result, she ended up being quite late. You just can't assume that a GPS always knows what it's talking about! I didn't mind though. It gave me time to sit and collect my thoughts.

Anyway, to continue the funny story, I eventually heard a car pull up so went out the front of the house to greet my guest. Now it was my turn to realise that assumptions sometimes take you by surprise. I was expecting a delicate English rose to emerge from her car, instead, a sturdy African protea did! There you go, so I assumed that a lady with an English accent and a French sounding name would be delicate and white, instead she was sturdy and black. I laughed inside thinking how foolish I'd been. If we were to adopt from Africa one day, our child would be black with an Aussie accent! The accent can't always tell you what someone might look like, right?

Well, we had an amicable chat over a cup of tea, then walked around the house and sheds looking for potential safety hazards or concerns. It was all pretty straight forward, and I felt confident that this lady would be a wonderful support if we were approved to foster.

Thankfully, we were allowed to supply our adoption assessment to DCP so we wouldn't have to go through another detailed probing and deeply personal interview. They are so draining. We had to do a few courses to help us understand our role and the state's role in fostering, along with courses about the impacts of interrupted infant attachment and trauma in the life of a child. Much of it was hard going. So many sad stories of children whose lives had got off to a terrible start and who needed so much care and support just to be able to relax and enjoy being in a family. We hoped and prayed we might be able to help a few children to understand what it means to love and trust adults. It's a big call that all foster carers must do their best to work towards. That goal is almost impossible to achieve in any meaningful way if you are only fostering children for short periods of time. How can you help a child to trust you if they're only with you for a couple of days? And that was what we had applied for, to be respite foster carers. That meant that we would only have children for a day or two, maybe a week at most. We decided that since we were waiting to adopt, we shouldn't foster long term as it could be interrupted at any time with a phone call saying there was a child who needed us to adopt them.

Well, we were approved after a couple of months (much quicker than adoption I might add) and very quickly were asked if we could foster a one-year-old boy and his toddler sister! We received a phone call mid-Thursday afternoon asking if we could look after them. It was a bit unexpected as it had been explained to us that we would most likely be called on to do planned regular respite which would be on the weekends! I guess we did say we would do some emergency care as well though. As it was too late to organise anyone else to take my place at Boys Brigade, I picked them up, and just brought them along. It was a bit chaotic and tiring having a couple of young ones who had no idea what a routine looked like. Meal-time routine? What's that? Bath time routine? What's that? Story time routine? What's that? Bedtime routine? WHAT'S THAT?!

Chapter 19

Fostering Stories

Over the next six months we provided respite or short-term care for six children ranging in age from 1 year old to 14. This was a challenging time in so many ways, as we grappled with the quirks of the government department and in some cases our own naivety. We had stipulated that we would only be willing to foster young children who are not yet in school. Given we home-schooled our own sons, we felt it would be highly disruptive to be doing school runs into Geraldton twice a day! A social worker from the department made it clear, however, that we needed to be firm and stand our ground, as we would certainly receive requests outside our stipulation. I think it was the second request which was already outside our parameters! A 14-year-old autistic boy whose mum was in hospital and had no family to look after him. The department explained that he wasn't doing very well in school and that they would be happy for him to be absent from school while he was with us. Well, I guess we could do that! How sad that a person would have no one to turn to when they needed some help to look after their son. Not a family member, not a friend, not a colleague, no one. It made me realise just how blessed

I was. My extended family all lived more than 350km away, but I knew I could call on them and they would do whatever they could to help. Not to mention my church family who, at the drop of a hat, would pull out all the stops to support us if we needed it. Being a Christian means, among many things, being in a loving family. This foster boy's mum didn't have any of that. So we took him on for a while. At first, he really didn't want to be with us. Eventually though, when Nic offered to teach him to drive in our old farm ute, he didn't want to go home! After a few short days, his mum was out of hospital and he was returned home, reluctantly on his part.

Our next placement was an adorable little 3-year-old boy. He was so sweet and gentle, and so sad to be away from his mum and dad. It seemed his parents really loved him and cared for him, but after doing something silly one time he was taken away from them. They were mortified and extremely remorseful. Again, after only a few days the sweet boy was returned to his parents who I think had learnt their lesson. Whatever they did to cause their son to be removed, I don't think they would do again!

Then came the real challenge, a 13-year-old boy. Hmm, school age. Well, he was only going to be with us for a couple of days, so school wasn't going to be an issue. We agreed, but the couple of days became a week, then two, then three, etc. He was a quiet young man with a very winning smile. The smile, however, hid a world of trauma. What difference could we really make in a young man's life in such a short time? He readily came to church with us, and when we gave him a Bible as a gift, he was so pleased. But something was niggling away inside him, and he started on a downward trajectory which everyone around him was powerless to stop. One weekend we had another foster boy join us. That was a mistake. On their own they were both ok, but together they were a world of trouble! Nic was away with a couple of our boys on a Boys Brigade camp, so I had them on my own. I sure was glad when that weekend was over. I've never coped well with overt defiance, and swearing and raised voices set me on edge. There was a bit of that over that weekend. It was quieter when we went back to just the one lad, but something was terribly wrong, and we could only watch as his life spiralled out of control. First, he wagged school, then he ran away, and the police had to bring him back, then he ended up in hospital having smoked something nasty for the first time.

He wanted to live somewhere else and eventually the department agreed to find a place for him with relatives. It was less than ideal, but there wasn't anything to do. How heartbreaking to see such a lovely young lad go so far down over only five short weeks.

Over the period that we were fostering, we saw a marked decline in the health of my mum. She had experienced a mild stroke a few years before and then later was diagnosed with Alzheimer's disease, a progressive mental deterioration brought on by a general degeneration of the brain. Although for many, the progression of this condition is slow, to us it seemed obvious that in mum's case it wasn't going to be that way. The challenge of balancing home-schooling, volunteering, fostering and frequent visits to Perth to visit with Mum became too much to bear and we decided that we needed to put a pause on fostering. It was during this time that I wrote a Psalm to the Lord.

Holding on to you, what else can I do?
My life is in your hands, Jesus help me stand
You're holding on to me, though I cannot see
What I need to do, so I trust in you

Holy Lord, Living Word, Breath of Life, You are God
In this changing world you stay the same
From the first to last you never change
You're the rock on which I stand

BROKEN DREAMS IN WOUNDED HANDS

Forgive my wondering soul, Jesus bring me home
My hope is found in you, nothing else will do
The tide is rushing in, the world is steeped in sin
But the world will fade away and your word it will remain

Holy Lord, Living Word, Breath of Life, You are God
In this changing world you stay the same
From the first to last you never change
You're the rock on which I stand

Help me reach the lost, no matter what the cost
To speak the truth in love with wisdom from above
Though trials will grip my life; persecutions strife
your grace is all I need, I'll cling to you indeed

Holy Lord, Living Word, Breath of Life, You are God
In this changing world you stay the same
From the first to last you never change
You're the rock on which I stand

In the midst of all the turmoil of our lives we received our update paperwork that needed to be completed to maintain our adoption approval. We hadn't heard anything from South Africa in the last two years, and Mandy could only inform us that there was no new information and that she didn't know if or when any information would be forthcoming. We had a huge decision before us.

Chapter 20

Broken Dreams in Wounded Hands

I remember it as clearly as if it were yesterday; I was sitting on the bed in my mum and dad's spare room just outside their granny flat, staring at a blank page of the notebook on my lap. I just didn't think I could do it again. The pile of paperwork, the application for a police clearance, the medical check-up to prove that we were still fit and healthy... the waiting; it was all too much. Remember the song I started writing to our adopted children many years before, while I still had hope? (See chapter 12) It was called "Worth the Wait". I'd penned those words while I was helplessly waiting, and was fully expecting I would finish the song when I held our new child in my arms. Although I couldn't complete it at the time, I was so sure that one day I would complete it and it would be a treasure to our child. But it had been 13 long years since we first enquired to Shepherds Keep about adoption and I was now almost 44 years old and felt the weight of all the troubles of those years. I will always rejoice that the Lord blessed me with four amazing sons and my love for them has only grown day by day. I had so much more love to give, but it wasn't to be that

BROKEN DREAMS IN WOUNDED HANDS

I would be able to give it to any more children of our own. Nic and I had the hard and tearful conversation about adoption, and decided that it was time to close the door on this chapter of our lives.

I had prayed from the start that if the Lord kept opening the doors, we would keep walking through them. We had thought many times before that the door was about to close, but so often it was unexpectedly flung open again. This time was different. The door was still open. We could fill in the paperwork for the fifth or sixth time and keep walking through, or we could grip the handle and gently close the door for ourselves. We were both so weary and couldn't see any light at the end of the tunnel. We prayed and felt God's peace, whatever decision we chose to make. With his hand covering ours, we eased the door shut. I cannot explain what I felt at that time. Numb? Yes. Broken? Yes. Loved by God and enveloped in his eternal arms? Yes, yes, yes. I closed my eyes and saw myself carrying this mangled broken thing in my worn-out hands. It was my dream of adoption. Notice it was my dream, not God's. I was hunched over and weeping. A hand reached out for me and squeezed my shoulder then let go. Through blurry eyes I looked up enough to see a man standing in white with his hands together, both stretched out to me with palms up. The hands had been wounded. The pain of those wounds must have been great. I somehow knew that I could place that mangled broken thing in these hands. That they would carry it for me and that somehow it was going to be okay.

I looked at the page in front of me again, picked up a pencil and, with tears freely falling, began to write a new Psalm:

> *Once young with life ahead, with hopes and dreams unsaid*
> *Each day was fresh and new, I trusted then in you*
> *But life's not always kind, some dreams I had in mind*
> *Slipped slowly from my hands, I'll never understand*

BROKEN DREAMS IN WOUNDED HANDS

But you call me now to trust, in the one who holds my heart
As I look to you I find, you were there right from the start.

And I place my broken dreams in wounded hands
Though my heart is broke I know you have a plan
Yes I place my broken dreams in Jesus' hands
For your ways are higher than the will of man

I've prayed your kingdom come, and that your will be done
But now I face the test, was I sincere in my request?
I've searched deep in my soul, to find my only goal
Was to love you my life through, and to serve Lord only you

So I hold on to your grace, that's sufficient for each day
I will choose to follow you, for your love will light the way

And I place my broken dreams in wounded hands
Though my heart is broke I know you have a plan
Yes I place my broken dreams in Jesus hands
For your ways are higher than the will of man

Jesus loves me this I know, for the Bible tells me so,
I am his, to him belong; though I'm weak, he is so strong.
Yes Jesus loves me, yes Jesus loves me, yes Jesus loves me
The Bible tells me so.

So I place my broken dreams in wounded hands
Though my heart is broke I know he has a plan
Yes I place my broken dreams in Jesus' hands
For his ways are higher than the will of man

BROKEN DREAMS IN WOUNDED HANDS

Jesus loves me this I know
Jesus loves me this I know
Jesus loves me this I know
Jesus loves me this I know

Chapter 21

Hope – In What?

Hope is a funny thing, isn't it? Without it, life is a sorry state of affairs. Even with it, life can be very tough, especially if our hope is focussed on all the wrong things. If I've learnt anything from this whole experience, it's that there is only One in whom I should place my hope, and if I do I will never have cause for despair. I may experience disappointment, sadness, failure, difficulties, and even grief, but in the end I will still have hope. And it's all tied in with faith. Scripture states that, "faith is being sure of what we hope for and certain of what we do not see." (Hebrews 11:1, NIV, 1984). Faith gives certainty to hope, and faith is a gift of God (Eph 2:8-10). We just have to receive it. Wow! Double wow! I must then ask myself, have I received God's gift of faith, or do I just talk about it without experiencing its reality in my life? I can say one thing for sure - I'm learning. Learning to look more to the Lord and less to my circumstances, learning to throw my hopes and dreams on him, learning to accept the gift and stop trying to earn it. Notice I emphasised that I'm learning? Hoping only in the Lord and his purposes is a lifelong journey and, I'm sorry to say,

I'm not too near to getting it right; but by God's grace and in his time, I'm closer every day.

I started out writing my story about eight years into our adoption journey because I felt so helpless and just wanted to DO something. I thought it might be a good memoir for our adopted children, so they could see how much we wanted them and fought for them, but when we drew the line under adoption, I didn't really know what to do with it. The original title was going to be 'Worth the Wait', the title of the song I started to write but never completed. This story was supposed to have ended in a joyous trip to Africa to bring our new children home, instead it ended in a broken heart just clinging on to Jesus. Who would want to read about that?

I now know the Lord works as much in the broken moments as in the joyous ones, maybe even more. When this truth dawned on me, I knew I had to finish writing my story. Surely I'm not the only one who has had dreams, good dreams, God-honouring dreams, which never came to fulfilment or were somehow shattered by the fallen world we live in. This then is for you, so you will know that the Lord is not finished with you. He sees your heart, and I believe is much more interested in shaping you to be more like Jesus than in fulfilling your dreams. So what do you really want? To be like Jesus, or to have your human dreams, hopes and longings fulfilled?

There is an old song we used to sing at church when I was a child:

> *To be like Jesus, to be like Jesus*
> *All I ask, to be like him*
> *All through life's journey from earth to glory*
> *all I ask, to be like him.*

©Public Domain

HOPE - IN WHAT?

Jesus himself said to his disciples, "If anyone would come after me, let him deny himself and take up his cross and follow me. For whoever would save his life will lose it, but whoever loses his life for my sake will find it" (Matthew 16:24-25, ESV). These are hard words if we're really going to put them into practice. But the Christian life is hard. If we're going to follow Jesus as he asks, it will be. But in all the trials and tribulations, in all the ups and downs, we have these words of Christ to cling to, "In this world you will have trouble. But take heart! I have overcome the world" (John 16:33, NIV).

My life in Christ is about bringing him glory; the outcomes of my actions are totally up to him. I won't ever give up on trying to 'do good' for the Lord. Scripture tells us to, "..not become weary in doing good, for at the proper time we will reap a harvest if we do not give up" (Galatians 6:9, NIV). I might not see the harvest on this side of eternity, but I will set my heart on things above, "where Christ is, seated at the right hand of God." I will set my mind on things above, not on earthly things, for I died, and my life is now hidden with Christ in God. When Christ, who is my life appears, then I also will appear with him in glory (Colossians 3:1-3, NIV).

I don't know your story, but I invite you to fix your eyes on Christ and hold tightly to the sure hope of eternal life with Him. Place your broken dreams in his wounded hands, and see what He will do.

Lord I need you every day, every moment, all the way
I can't stand up on my own, all my life is but a groan
Lord you are my strength and shield, you're the one to whom I yield
O I need you Saviour, Friend; 'til my life comes to an end

O my soul find rest in God, look to him, look above
All the worries of our time, for in him is peace sublime

BROKEN DREAMS IN WOUNDED HANDS

So on Christ I'll take my stand, moving on at his command
Only forward, ever on; 'til I reach my heavenly home

> *Lord I need you every day, every moment all the way*
> *When the clouds of doubt roll in, when confronted with my sin*
> *Lord forgive my wandering soul, hold on tight, don't let me go*
> *My hope is found in you, you're my rock and my refuge*

O my soul find rest in God, look to him, look above
All the worries of our time, for in him is peace sublime
So on Christ I'll take my stand, moving on at his command
Only forward, ever on; 'til I reach my heavenly home

> *Lord I need you every day, every moment all the way*
> *In the sunshine in the rain, to live is Christ, to die is gain*
> *Christ my rock and my salvation, yes in him I'll not be shaken*
> *When I see him face to face, then I'll know I've run the race*

O my soul find rest in God, look to him, look above
All the worries of our time, for in him is peace sublime
So on Christ I'll take my stand, moving on at his command
Only forward, ever on; 'til I reach my heavenly home

Only forward, ever on; 'til I reach my heavenly home.

Amen.

Epilogue

Today is Monday the 25th of July 2022. As I write I'm sitting in our office in our home in Kununurra. This time last year, Nic, Darcy, Justin and I came on a camping trip in the northern end of WA (doing the Gibb River Road if that means anything to anyone!), with my sister Kathryn, her husband Darren and most of their family. As it happened, during the trip Nic and I had our 25th wedding anniversary. To celebrate, we left Darcy and Justin with the others and took a detour to Kununurra and while there we visited a ministry called 'Reach Beyond'. The vision of Reach Beyond is, 'to see Jesus known and loved by unreached people' and its mission is to 'transform the lives of individuals and communities by using dynamic media and community development initiatives that serve as the Voice and Hands of Jesus'. We had previously heard of the work of Reach Beyond in broadcasting gospel and community development programs to unreached people groups through their short-wave radio transmitters in Kununurra and we were keen to tour their site. Although we had missed the organised tour, one of the staff agreed to show us around. We were pretty impressed by their set up. Through radio they were reaching about 24 unreached people groups (in their own languages), and locally in Kununurra they were partnered with Alta-1 College which provides life-changing education to 'at risk' high school students in need of support.

BROKEN DREAMS IN WOUNDED HANDS

It was an interesting way to celebrate our anniversary (we also visited the famous Lake Argyle and had a scrumptious dinner at the local Country Club!), but it was certainly a God incidence. Let's make a long story short. Reach Beyond was looking for a new Operations Manager for their facilities in Kununurra and Nic felt compelled to apply for the position. After having a long conversation with the CEO, a family meeting, and concerted prayer on both our parts, Nic applied for the position. What do you know? he got it! So here we are, 3000km away from our home and family in Greenough/Perth, serving the Lord in Kununurra. His ways are certainly higher than our ways, and his thoughts than our thoughts. When I began writing my story, I would never have predicted that as I finished it I would be so far from home, supporting Nic as he serves in a full time practical ministry position. But God knows my heart for missions. He always has, and he always will. He knows which dreams he will fulfil and which ones he will lay aside. I look forward to whatever he has in store with open hands, and pray for the grace to receive any dream that the Lord will place in them.

www.ingramcontent.com/pod-product-compliance
Lightning Source LLC
Chambersburg PA
CBHW022107090426
42743CB00008B/745